T0329026

THE PRIMITIVE
CHRISTIAN CATECHISM

THE PRIMITIVE CHRISTIAN CATECHISM

A Study in the Epistles

BY

PHILIP CARRINGTON

M.A. (Cantab.), Lit.D. (N.Z.)
Hon. S.T.D., Hon. D.C.L.
Bishop of Quebec

CAMBRIDGE
AT THE UNIVERSITY PRESS
1940

CAMBRIDGE
UNIVERSITY PRESS

University Printing House, Cambridge CB2 8BS, United Kingdom

Cambridge University Press is part of the University of Cambridge.

It furthers the University's mission by disseminating knowledge in the pursuit of education, learning and research at the highest international levels of excellence.

www.cambridge.org
Information on this title: www.cambridge.org/9781107448223

© Cambridge University Press 1940

First published 1940
First paperback edition 2014

A catalogue record for this publication is available from the British Library

ISBN 978-1-107-44822-3 Paperback

To
MY FATHER

PREFACE

The author was prevented from carrying these studies any further by becoming Bishop of the great missionary Diocese of Quebec with its two hundred and eighty thousand square miles of territory. He has, however, been urged to publish his researches and conclusions, even though in many respects they have not been fully worked out. This procedure has involved a restriction of scope which is probably beneficial, though it has precluded a detailed study of the texts in the light of the general thesis, or a full study of the allied literature whether Jewish or Christian.

In the case of late Hebrew, he must confess that he is not equipped to make a first-hand investigation, and has had to rely on English and German literature which often leaves much to be desired. He has not been able, for instance, to find a translation of *Sifra* to Leviticus into a modern language, or any critical discussion or commentary on it. When one considers that Leviticus was the first reader used in Jewish education, and that *Sifra* sheds light on how it was understood in the second, and probably the first, century A.D., it will be realised how far we are yet from a true appreciation of the cultural background of the Jewish Christianity which gave birth to the religion of the New Testament. An attempt has, however, been made in Chapter I to indicate some features of the traditional mode of education in what I have called the 'old piety'. Chapter II deals with the introduction of the proselyte into the circle of levitical Judaism, and suggests that there are clear traces in the New Testament that this procedure has influenced the earliest Christian mission in its handling of gentile converts, thereby producing formulae which may be described as neo-levitical.

Chapter III takes one or two passages from I Peter which have been explained as borrowings from the Pauline epistles,

PRIMITIVE CHRISTIAN CATECHISM

and argues that this explanation is unlikely. They are best explained as traditional catechetical material of Jewish character, used independently by each writer. This forms the starting-point of the New Testament investigation.

Chapter IV deals with other formulae which are common to all three authors. Four points common to Ephesians (Colossians), I Peter, and James form the basis of the study; as they tend to occur in the same order, at the same logical position, and with the same effect, it is thought justifiable to allude to them as a pattern. The passages which form this pattern are, it is contended, of a catechetical nature, and are connected with baptism. Chapter V deals with the vocabulary of the pattern, which is held to be more characteristic of catechetical documents than of the New Testament writers who preserve it. Chapter VI treats of the thought sequence of the pattern when isolated from the documents which contain it.

The reader may regard some of the evidence as slight and inconclusive; but the fact remains that the resemblances do exist, and that they tend to occur in the same order. The four points are no more than a basis for study; the reader who rejects the significance of one or more of them will himself find others (to which I also allude) which may impress him more. The total range of resemblances calls for some explanation; the theory of literary borrowing from the Pauline writing is inadmissible; in some shape or form the theory of a common pattern or storehouse of catechetical material seems bound to take its place. It is hoped that the thesis advanced in this little book may have some value as a preliminary exploration in the work of discussing the common pattern.

It may be added that the minor resemblances call for as careful study as the major resemblances, and may, when understood, prove equally illuminating. Unless all are dismissed as coincidence (which I cannot conceive possible), all must be equally taken into consideration.

Assuming the truth of the theory which has been advanced, I go on, in Chapter VII, to indicate some respects in which

⟨ viii ⟩

apostolic and post-apostolic Christianity developed on the same lines as rabbinic Judaism. Chapter VIII attempts to show how the four epistles fit into such a system. Chapter IX returns to the pattern and expounds it (with some use of conjecture) as a baptismal ritual, or as a series of didactic formulae connected with the baptismal rite.

The true test of a theory of this kind is subsequent to the establishment of its probability by detailed examination of textual evidence. It lies in the way in which it illuminates the situation as a whole, especially problems which had not been taken into account in evolving the theory.

One such problem, in this case, is the high importance of the epistles in the early canon. The nature of apostolic Christianity was not such as to account for this on purely literary grounds; but if the epistles were the principal authoritative transcripts of the kind of oral teaching which was employed in the catechetical instruction of converts, we can understand at once their vital importance, and the pre-eminent position which they occupy in the mind of such a writer as St Polycarp.

Similarly the use of the epistle as a mode of authoritative intervention by an apostolic *tannā* (teacher) in an actual ecclesiastical situation is clearly carried on into the sub-apostolic age, till the period when the accepted epistles begin to be thought of as Scripture in their own right possessing a primary value as sacred literature. In the subapostolic age letters from St Clement, St Ignatius, or St Polycarp still have something of the effect of a letter from St Paul, St Peter, or St John (even though it may be disclaimed).

Again, the idea of a 'tannaite' succession of elders, as in contemporary Judaism, adds something to our understanding of the growth of what is called apostolic succession.

Another important point is concerned with the origin of the rites of catholic baptism which have been attributed by various scholars to Mandaean sources, mystery religions, or other pagan influences. If the conjectural exposition of the apostolic pattern attempted in Chapter IX is admitted to have any validity, we begin to see the possibility of an apostolic baptismal rite which could be the ancestor of the historical catholic rite, and yet trace its own ancestry to Jewish practice. It must be owned that such a process of continuous development is more acceptable than the violent discontinuity demanded by some present-day theories.

The author desires to express his thanks to his friends the Rev. F. C. Grant, late Dean of the Seabury-Western Seminary, Evanston, Illinois, and now professor in the Union Theological Seminary, New York, and the Rev. A. H. Forster, Librarian of the Hibbard Old Testament Library, who read the MS. of this book in a much more extended form; to the Rev. B. S. Easton for sympathy and encouragement, and for library facilities at the General Theological Seminary, New York; also to the Rev. Kenneth Naylor of the Diocesan College, Montreal, for assistance and encouragement, especially in the later stages of production.

PHILIP QUEBEC

Easter 1938

CONTENTS

PRIMITIVE CHRISTIAN CATECHISM

TABLES

CHAPTER I
TŌRĀH IN ISRAEL

SUMMARY OF CHAPTER I

Religious instruction among the Jews in New Testament times was oral, traditional, and semi-ritual.

Its subject-matter was *tōrāh* (instruction, discipline, law), *ḥokmāh* (wisdom), and *halākāh* (walking).

Its ministers (apart from the priestly *tōrāh*) were the fathers or elders; when teachers were evolved, they spoke of themselves as fathers and elders, and professed a genealogical descent (succession). They exercised divine authority.

The principal occasions of instruction were (1) Passover—e.g. Exod. xii–xxiv, *Mekilta*, the Haggadah ritual, etc., (2) Synagogue assembly—e.g. Lev. xvii ff., etc., (3) Rabbinic schools—e.g. Ecclus. i–vii, *Two Ways, Aboth*, etc.

These represent the old piety which had no conception of future rewards and punishments, etc. The new piety may be studied in *Testaments, Mandata*, etc.

The old piety presupposes a religious-social group set apart and indwelt by a divine presence.

CHAPTER I

TŌRĀH IN ISRAEL

1. The word *tōrāh* in Israel is a correlative of *ḥokmāh* (wisdom) and means instruction rather than law in the sense in which we understand law. It is connected, not with theological or speculative knowledge, but with behaviour or 'walking'—*halākāh*; the wise man knows how to conduct himself in relation to the Lord, and to the religious-social unit of which he is a member.

2. The body of *tōrāh* exists in a traditional form of which analogous cases may be studied in various primitive communities, such as the Maoris of New Zealand, who handed down a complicated system of myth, history, ritual, and custom, in a purely oral manner, writing being unknown to them.[1] Transcripts of these traditions were made in the nineteenth century, by means of which a reliable history of some seven centuries has been constructed, and an outline which, it is said, may go back more than two thousand years. The first six books of the Old Testament are transcripts of similar traditions, and we ought not to assume that the oral tradition ceased to function when the transcript was made, or even that the written transcript then became primary. The transcript may be regarded as a cross-section of the living tradition at a given time and place. It is necessary to remember these principles also in the study of the New Testament literature.

3. The word 'tradition' is only applicable to a permanent and accepted element within the public life of a community;[2] and no tradition can be understood without reference to the conditions of life in the community. In primitive conditions of life, the mode of thought in connection with the tradition of wisdom is genealogical. Though from one point of view a

1 Cf. *The Lore of the Whare Whananga*, T. Percy Smith.
2 Even an esoteric tradition can occupy an official position.

remarkable degree of rigidity and permanence is achieved in the outward form of the tradition, it has to be remembered that it is a living biological phenomenon.

4. In Israel the simplest picture is that of the father handing on to the son the *tōrāh* which he had received from his father.[1] As this *tōrāh* is thought of as ultimately coming from God, it follows that the father has a godlike status in reference to the son, and the honour paid to parents is a form of the honour paid to God.[2] The fifth commandment belongs to the first table of the law;[3] and in other formulae the honour of parents comes next after the fear of the Lord.[4] This godlike status is extended to the elders of the tribe, who are, of course, the fathers of the tribe.[5] When a professional class of teachers comes into existence we find them assuming this divine father-son relationship as the basis of their teaching;[6] and in course of time a genealogical succession of teachers is developed.[7] Its early stages may be studied in Proverbs and Ecclesiasticus where the pupils do not yet seem to use books; its final development may be seen in the New Testament

---

1 Prov. i, 1–8, iv, 1–4, etc. Tobit iv is an excellent example of paternal *tōrāh*. The death-bed blessings of Jacob and Tobit are examples of a special form of this *tōrāh*, the 'testament'. *The Testament of the Twelve Patriarchs* makes use of the same literary form (as it has now become) to provide a paternal *tōrāh* for Israel as a whole.

2 Mal. i, 6 argues from this likeness of status. Cf. Ecclus. iii, 1–16. In the Mishnah, Kid. 30b says that the honour and fear given to parents is equal to that given to God. Peah 15d says, 'When a man honours his father and mother, the Holy One, blessed be he, says, I ascribe it as though I dwelt with them and was honoured.'

3 The tables are so divided in *Mekilta* and elsewhere. The honour of parents is part of the fear of the Lord. Cf. Pseudo-Phocylides, i, 8: 'First honour God, and next to that thy parents.'

4 Eph. vi, 2 calls it the 'first commandment with promise' (i.e. of long life and of children). In many codes it *is* the first commandment, following the inculcation of the fear of the Lord or other prefatory matter; note its early position in Ps.-Phoc., Lev. xix, 3, Prov. i, 7, Mal. i, 6, Ecclus. iii, 1–16, Tob. iv, 3, etc. In Rom. xiii, 1ff., I Pet. ii, 17, etc., the words 'fear' and 'honour' are to be explained from this mode of thought.

5 Lev. xix, 32, etc. See p. 67, n. 3.

6 E.g. 'Who teaches *tōrāh* to the son of his fellowman, has it ascribed to him as though he had begotten him" (Sanh. 19b).

7 In Prov. iv, 1ff. and Ecclus. iii, 1 this seems to be already the case.

period (cf. *Pirke Aboth*),[1] where reference is made to the written law which is now studied by the pupils. Ecclesiasticus is a transcript of a fully oral system; *Pirke Aboth* is a transcript of an oral scholasticism, based on scripture, and embodied in a didactic succession.

5. Many phenomena of the New Testament period are best explained by the assumption that elementary education of converts in religious duties was not given from books, but from oral catechisms like those of which we possess transcripts in the *Gnomai*[2] of Phocylides, the *Two Ways*[3] (or *Way of Life*) embodied in *Barnabas* and *Didache*, the *Mandata* of Hermas,[4] and similar literature. The real repositories of knowledge and wisdom are the 'wise' ('elders' and 'teachers'); where books exist, they are still mere transcripts. It is at once obvious that this conception may be fruitfully applied to the Gospels and Epistles. The Sermon on the Mount is such a transcript of the *tōrāh* of the Lord as it was taught by the elders of the Christian community; it is itself a new form of the oral *tōrāh* of Israel to which, in the Matthaean version, constant reference is made.[5]

1 *Pirke Aboth* contains sayings of Rabbis many of whom are contemporary with the New Testament writers. It is easily accessible in the Hebrew Prayer-Book or Danby's *Mishnah*.

2 It seems impossible to date the *Gnomai*, which is a collection of counsels in morals and religion, written in Greek hexameters, but drawn mostly from Jewish sources. Text in Bergk, *Anthologia Lyrica*.

3 The *Two Ways* was a catechism of the Greek synagogue based on Hebrew sources, and incorporated into two Christian documents called *The Teaching of the Twelve Apostles* and the *Epistle of Barnabas*. My quotations are from the former (cited as Didache or Did.) and have the support of the latter unless otherwise stated. It is my opinion that the second 'way' (of death or darkness) is a later addition, and that the catechism was originally merely the *Way of Life*. A shorter form may have been known to the author of the *Apology of Aristides*.

4 The writings of the Roman prophet Hermas were probably composed at intervals between about A.D. 95 and the accession of his brother Pius as bishop of Rome (about 140?). The *Muratorian Fragment* tells us that a compilation of them (*conscripsit*) was made during his episcopate to be read in church. The second part of these writings (*Mandata*, i.e. Commandments) is mainly composed of Jewish catechetical material closely allied to passages in James, Ephesians, and the *Two Ways*.

5 Matt. v, 17 ff., vii, 12.

PRIMITIVE CHRISTIAN CATECHISM

6. There were, of course, special circumstances under which *tōrāh* was given; for instruction in the 'fear of the Lord' was a feature of the life of the holy community.

1. *Passover*

7. The paschal meal is the holiest point in family life in Israel, and the occasion on which the father instructs the son in the great *haggādāh* (instruction-narrative) of the Exodus, so that the festival itself may be alluded to as the Haggadah. A study of *Mekilta*[1] suggests that the original narrative of Exod. xii–xxiv had itself an instructional and initiatory character; it was certainly so regarded in the New Testament period. Beginning with the passover ritual[2] and the blood of the covenant, *Mekilta* develops the thought of Israel turning from idolatry, and, by the Red Sea baptism, becoming the son of God; it stresses the faith of Israel, and the gift of the Holy Spirit through which Israel was enabled to sing the song of triumph;[3] it goes on to the appointment of elders, the ten Commandments, and the covenant sacrifice. St Paul, in I and II Corinthians, is clearly working from a midrash of this character.[4] This *haggādāh*, relating to the initiation of Israel as God's son, is used for instructional purposes at the paschal festival which is also the occasion of the instruction (and initiation?) of the son within the family,[5] and perhaps

---

1 *Mekilta* is a 'midrash' to this part of Exodus. It is said to have received its earliest (literary?) form under R. Akiba in the first quarter of the second century A.D. German translation by Windisch and Wunsch.

2 The passover meal re-enacts the Exodus story, which was the moment when Israel turned from idolatry to God, and became his 'son'. The 'blood of the covenant' in which this was done has three major associations which are linked together in *Mekilta*, (a) the escape from Egypt, (b) circumcision, (c) the covenant sacrifice at Sinai; from this usage it passes into the similar Christian tradition, I Cor. xi, 25, etc.

3 Compare with this sequence from *Mekilta* the Christian sequence of faith, baptism, the reception of the Holy Spirit, and the gift of tongues which includes song (I Cor. xiv, 15). *Mekilta*, like St Paul, insists on the faith of Abraham, and, like St James, refers to the offering of Isaac.

4 I Cor. x, etc. Cf. 'Now all these things happened unto them for ensamples, and were written for our admonition' (x, 11).

5 Exod. xii, 26, xiii, 14.

also the admission of the gēr or stranger into the congregation of Israel.[1] It should be remembered that initiation, instruction, and education are aspects of one process in the primitive culture.

8. We have in the passover a living tradition of great antiquity of which very different cross-sections are preserved in Exod. xii–xxiv, *Mekilta*, *Tractate Pesachim*, and even perhaps in I and II Corinthians which seem to be in parts at least derived from a passover paraenesis.[2]

2. *The Synagogue*

9. As S. Krauss[3] points out, the word *'ēdāh* means nothing at all but the Israelite community duly gathered under its proper officials, the elders; he follows A. Rosenmann in deriving the historical institution known as a synagogue in New Testament times from the *ma'amad*, or standing congregation of lay Israelites who met in the Hall Gazzit of the temple at Jerusalem in order to take part at the door of the sanctuary in the daily sacrifices.[4] It is difficult to see how this institution in Jerusalem could have given rise to other synagogues throughout Israel; but if we admit (which he is unwilling to do) that other sanctuaries persisted into a late period, the local synagogues would (on his own hypothesis) be the gathering of the local community at the door of the local sanctuary.[5] Even when sacrifice was abolished at the local sanctuaries, there would still be many purposes which such sanctuaries would serve;[6] and if the local community had been in the habit of meeting there, there is no reason to

1 *Pesachim*, viii, 8 gives an example of this.
2 E.g. I Cor. v, 7 f., and xv, 20. The ceremony of the 'firstfruits' occurs in passover week. Parts of I Peter also suggest passover; see p. 28, n. 1.
3 *Synagogale Altertümer*.
4 As demanded in Lev. iv, 15.
5 I am pleased to see, since writing this, that S. A. Cook in his recent book, *The Old Testament*, p. 148, also suggests that the synagogues represent the old sanctuaries.
6 There are traces of their continued use in the Mishnah; e.g. Meg. i, 11 contemplates offering certain types of sacrifice at a high place; Megillah also deals with synagogues.

PRIMITIVE CHRISTIAN CATECHISM

suppose they would cease to do so. Such a state of affairs might explain the well-known allusion in Ps. lxxiv, 8. It seems, too, the best way of explaining the actual arrangements of the synagogues, the ritual door, the elders 'with their backs to the sanctuary', and the presence of priests.[1] The synagogue is often called a secondary sanctuary, or simply a sanctuary.

10. Neh. viii and I Esdras ix, 37 ff.[2] give us a picture of a synagogue type of service at the door of the Jerusalem temple; but in earlier times sacred instruction seems to be a function of the priesthood.[3] This seems to be the situation presupposed in the Holiness Code (H) of Leviticus,[4] a code which is compatible with the existence of local sanctuaries. Certain parts of H are addressed to the people as well as to the priesthood, in particular Lev. xix, which is composed in stanzas with the refrain 'I am Yahweh your 'El'. This chapter, which covers most of the duties of religion in gnomic form, is the principal base of many subsequent catechisms,[5] in particular, of the *Zadokite Fragment*,[6] of

1 See Sukenik, *Ancient Synagogues*.
2 Two versions of the same narrative. Both, no doubt, were intended to supply a pattern for the synagogue service; but in I Esdras the pattern is more completely worked out, and forms the climax of the book.
3 See Mal. ii, 5–7. Malachi has frequent allusions to a code of *tōrāh* of a priestly type.
4 The Holiness Code is based on the conception of a holy community (Lev. xix, 2) indwelt by a holy God (xxvi, 11, 12) and characterised by mutual love (xix, 18) and submission to authority (xix, 32).
5 Hertz (*Pentateuch and Haftorahs*) says that it is stated in *Sifra* that Leviticus is the central book of the *tōrāh*, and that chapter xix is the central chapter of that book, and therefore of the whole *tōrāh*. Of this central chapter, verse 18 (love of one's neighbour) is called by R. Akiba, as well as by St Paul, the completion or summary of the law. According to Lev. R. vii, 3, children began their education with the study of Leviticus. We need not doubt that Leviticus, and especially Chapter xix, was fundamental in Jewish catechesis.
6 The *Zadokite Fragment* is the *tōrāh* of a peculiar sect, probably Samaritan, and, according to Charles, of the second century B.C. The Hebrew text is published by Schechter, and affords us a stage in *tōrāh* intermediate between the Old and New Testaments. English translation with commentary by R. H. Charles in *Apocrypha and Pseudepigrapha*. I fear, however, that Dr Charles' elucidation needs much revision; in

⟨ 8 ⟩

the *Gnomai*[1] of Phocylides, and even to some extent of the Sermon on the Mount.

3. *The Rabbinic School*

11. The *Wisdom of Ben Sirah* (Ecclesiasticus) provides us with a cross-section of the secular instruction given in the lay schools. It does not touch the specifically priestly *tōrāh* of sacrifice, clean and unclean, etc., though it shows devotion to the levitical system. Its subject is 'fear of the Lord', which signifies, as Hertz points out,[2] natural piety. The material of Chapters i–vii is used again and again in later writers, especially in the *Two Ways*, the *Mandata* of Hermas, and the Epistle of St James.

12. Each of these three types of tradition demands a peculiar social group within which it functions. The paschal tradition belongs to the family; the levitical tradition belongs to the tribe or holy congregation gathered in the presence of the Lord; the rabbinic tradition belongs to the school. But we must be careful to avoid the conception of a dry or humanistic didacticism; the learner coming to school is 'approaching' the fear of the Lord,[3] the teacher is endued with godlike honour,[4] and 'wisdom' is itself a grace from God; there is, in

particular the location of the sect in Damascus is an error; the *Fragment* is referring to the captivity of northern Israel 'beyond Damascus' (Amos v, 27: quoted in the *Fragment*), not to anything in its own time.

1 M. Dibelius, in his commentary on James in the Meyer series, has pointed out that Phocylides is a Greek form of Lev. xix. There is, of course, much other material.

2 *Pentateuch and Haftorahs* to Lev. xix, 2; but supernatural piety might be nearer the mark. The old piety of pre-Christian Judaism is love and fear of a *numen praesens*, not dictated ethics.

3 Ecclus. i, 28, ii, 1. In the levitical type of priestly *tōrāh*, the enquirer 'drew near to God' by approaching a sanctuary. The synagogue also was a sanctuary. The rabbinic teachers appear to have attempted to retain this sense of approaching a divine presence. Much apparently 'ethical' *tōrāh* is originally sanctuary *tōrāh*, like Ps. xv.

4 In *Mekilta* to Exod. xvii, 9, Aboth iv, 15, etc., it is said that the 'fear' of the teacher is as the 'fear' of God. The *Two Ways* (Did. iv, 1, but altered in Barn.) says, 'Him who speaketh unto thee the word of God, thou shalt honour as the Lord; for where the lordship is spoken of, there is the Lord.'

short, an element of real presence.[1] (On this point see W. Lockton, *Divers Orders of Ministers*.)

The New Piety

13. All three types are alike in looking only to this life for rewards and punishments; even the Sermon on the Mount is true to the old piety in this respect. But a new piety had actually arisen, though it had not as yet got possession of the schools, which spoke of destinies beyond the grave, of the Gan Eden and the Ge Hinnom. Whereas the old piety dealt with definite duties towards God and one's neighbour, with some stress on inward disposition (the 'heart'), the new piety dealt with abstract vices and virtues and with self-perfection. The old piety had indeed looked on wisdom as a 'spirit' or *dunamis* from the Lord, but the new refers much more frequently to other spiritual forces within or without the soul, and in particular to a contention between the forces of light and the forces of darkness which, while it occupies the whole universe, yet has its focal point in the soul.

14. The new ideas seem to have some affinity with Persian thought; we may be right in connecting them with Pharisaism; we note that they influence Christian literature in varying degrees, most strongly perhaps in St Paul and Hermas, much less in I Peter and the *Two Ways*. But the best monument of the new piety is the *Testaments of the Twelve Patriarchs*.

---

1 Aboth iii, 7, 'When ten people sit together, and occupy themselves with *tōrāh*, the *Shekinah* abides among them, etc.'

CHAPTER II
PROSELYTE BAPTISM

SUMMARY OF CHAPTER II

There is no need to assume the existence of proselyte catechisms other than the old catechetical material. The *Two Ways, Mandata,* etc., are probably old Hebrew material arranged for the Greek synagogue.

The *gēr* (convert from heathenism) was initiated into Israel by (a) baptism, (b) circumcision, (c) sacrifice. Proselyte baptism probably derived from the *tebīlāh* of Lev. xvii, 15.

Christian baptism appears to have been assimilated to Jewish proselyte baptism in the mission field.

Levitical conditions for Christian proselyte in (a) Acts xv, (b) I Thess. iv, and I Cor. v and vi, (c) I Pet. i. The Western text of Acts xv may be a summary of the tradition which is the base of (b) and (c).

An outline of the Christian tradition of walking (*halākāh*) or consecration:

(1) Not to walk as the gentiles: Lev. xviii, 1–5.

(2) To avoid the (three) major sins: Lev. xvii–xviii.

(3) The reception of the Spirit is a call to holiness: Lev. xix, 2.

(4) Love one another: Lev. xix, 18.

The Christian community is a sanctuary or temple in which is the presence of God, i.e. a new form of the holy levitical community (Lev. xxvi, 11–12).

PROSELYTE BAPTISM

1. The system of oral instruction by elders grew out of the primitive customs by which children were initiated into full membership in the tribe; the transcripts of this instruction are therefore to be compared to the catechism, of which they are the lineal ancestors. They were also used for 'proselytes', or converts from heathenism; but it seems a little rash to speak of proselyte catechisms, as if new forms were prepared for the use of proselytes. There is little in the Greek catechism material which we possess that seems unsuitable for use within Israel. The proselyte is as a little child, a statement which strongly suggests that he at once assumes child status in the instruction system.[1] In the New Testament, too, the convert has to go through a period of instruction in 'wisdom' and 'knowledge' before he reaches adult status ('perfection').

2. Greek texts, therefore, such as the *Two Ways* and the *Mandata*, are to be looked on as the catechetical material of the Greek synagogue designed for hearers or catechumens of all kinds, whether children or adult proselytes. It is a Greek recension of Hebrew material, much of which can be traced back to Lev. xix, Ecclus. vii, etc. It would appear likely that it is from the Greek synagogue that it passes into the Christian church; but the process should be thought of as the development of a living organism rather than the borrowing of a literature.

3. The Greek word proselyte (or epelyte) means 'comer', and represents the Hebrew word gēr, 'stranger', which in late Hebrew has the regular meaning of 'convert'. Both the paschal tōrāh (Exod. xii–xxiv) and the Holiness Code (Lev. xviiff.) have sections dealing with the status of the gēr. His

[1] It is difficult to see how anyone can enter a tribal community based on pedigree and consanguinity, except by a fictional birth, or adoption.

initiation into full membership of the Israelite community was marked by (*a*) baptism, (*b*) circumcision, (*c*) the offering of a sacrifice. Baptism was originally, it would seem, a preliminary rite which cleansed him from defilements due to neglect of the taboos of Lev. xvii and xviii, in which chapters the ceremony of total immersion (*tebīlāh*)[1] is prescribed. Gradually it assumed greater importance, until it became possible, in an academic disputation, for learned rabbis to argue that it was baptism, not circumcision, which made the convert an Israelite; the ritual states that he rises from the water an Israelite in all respects.[2]

Christian Baptism and Levitical Holiness

4. Christian baptism had, of course, a different origin, since it was first administered to Jews, though it, too, may have been originally suggested by the *tebīlāh* of Lev. xvii; but when Christianity entered the mission field, the rite was bound to assimilate itself to Jewish proselyte baptism. The stages are these:

(*a*) Pure Jewish Christianity.
(*b*) Greek-speaking Jewish Christianity.
(*c*) The appeal to non-Jews.

5. The controversies of A.D. 49 had to do with the status of non-Jews who had received Christian baptism. St Paul's view was that they were to be treated as Israelites; another party, associated with the name of St James, held that they must complete their initiation into Israel by means of circumcision, and go on to learn and observe the rest of the levitical *tōrāh*. A document preserved in Acts xv records and promulgates a decision which dispenses with circumcision and other levitical requirements, but demands that a certain standard of levitical purity be maintained by abstention (*apechesthai*—'to keep one's distance') from things offered to idols, from fornication,

1 Or *tebūl yōm*.
2 On proselyte baptism, see W. Brandt, *Die Jüdische Baptismen*, and F. L. Gavin, *Jewish Antecedents of the Christian Sacraments*; also B. S. Easton, *The Apostolic Tradition of Hippolytus*.

and from blood,[1] three points which may be taken to cover fairly well the contents of Lev. xvii and xviii, the introductory chapters of the Holiness Code.

6. An attempt has been made to show that these three taboos represent purely ethical conceptions; and it is true that in contemporary Judaism there is a triad of great sins, idolatry, fornication, and murder,[2] which 'profane the land', and 'cause the *shekīnāh* to depart'. But it is unwise to make an absolute distinction in this period between ethics and cultus. Both formulae probably represent the same tradition. In Acts the emphasis is on cultus; in the Rabbinic tradition less so; in both cases we are dealing with offences against a holy God indwelling a holy community, which is the picture of Lev. xix.

7. It would seem likely that, where the regulations of Acts xv were in force, special stress must have been laid before baptism on the renunciation of these three forms of uncleanness; and in other localities (Jewish as well as Christian) similar steps may have been taken. Phocylides prefixes to his paraphrase of Lev. xix four rhymed lines which forbid (among other things) wrong sexual acts, the shedding of blood, and also the cult of idols, if by *pseudea* he means idols.[3] In *Didache*, the prohibitions, which come early in the *Two Ways*, are much elaborated, in order to cover the same type of gentile sins; but much of the material included in these prohibitions is to be found in Lev. xvii–xix.

---

1 The short text seems to be original; the question of the precise historical value of Acts xv does not affect our argument.

2 An early form of the three major sins is found in the *Zadokite Fragment*, vi, 11; see notes by Charles *ad loc*. For a treatment of the rabbinic doctrine, see A. Büchler, *Studies in Sin and Atonement*. Compare the 'Noachic' taboos, perhaps for gentiles living as dependents in a Hebrew community. The subject is fully discussed in Lake and Jackson, *Beginnings of Christianity*.

3 Pseudo-Phoc. lines 3–7:

μήτε γαμοκλοπέειν, μήτ' ἄρσενα Κύπριν ὀρίνειν,
μήτε δόλους ῥάπτειν, μήθ' αἵματι χεῖρα μιαίνειν,
μὴ πλουτεῖν ἀδίκως ἀλλ' ἐξ ὁσίων βιοτεύειν...
ψεύδεα μὴ βάζειν, τὰ δ' ἐτήτυμα πάντ' ἀγορεύειν.

⟨ 15 ⟩

8. When we find, therefore, that the exhortations to the practice of piety in Colossians, Ephesians, and I Peter begin with an exhortation to 'walk' no longer 'according to the custom of the gentiles', we are led to suspect that this is a common catechetical opening, based originally on Lev. xviii, 1–5, 24–30, and similar passages.

Neo-levitical Formulae in Paul

9. In I Thessalonians, which was written by Paul, Silvanus, and Timothy, not long after the events narrated in Acts xv, reference is made to a Christian law of holiness ('your sanctification...how you ought to walk') which had already been taught to converts during a period of evangelisation which had only lasted a few weeks. It contains the exact phrase of the letter of Acts xv, to 'refrain (*apechesthai*[1]) from fornication'; and this is further explained as to 'know how to preserve his vessel in holiness and honour, not in passion of lust as the gentiles who know not God' (iv, 4–5). The next verse

> Not to over-reach
> Nor defraud his brother in the matter:
> For the Lord is the avenger...

echoes the style and matter of Lev. xix (cf. *v*. 11).

10. This negative aspect of consecration is reinforced in a positive way by the 'called...unto holiness' of *v*. 7, and the 'brotherly love' of *v*. 9, which recall Lev. xix, 2 and 18. The same sequence of thought occurs in I Peter where Lev. xix, 2 is actually quoted (i, 15); and comparison can be made with Rom. xii, 10 and Gal. v, 14 which quote Lev. xix, 18 (see Table I). The Western text of Acts xv, 29 gives still another similar sequence of formulae; for the three taboos are there followed by the golden rule in its negative form (cf. Tobit iv

---

1 ἀπέχεσθαι is only found in the New Testament in I Tim. iv, 3, except for the three parallel passages in Acts, I Peter, and I Thessalonians, from which we are attempting to make this reconstruction. It is also a curious fact that the name of Silvanus (Silas) is connected with each document.

and R. Hillel) which can logically be derived from Lev. xxiv,
19,[1] and then comes a reference to the Holy Spirit.

11. Though the levitical consecration language tends to
disappear in the later writings of St Paul, so that we must look
to the parallel in I Peter i for light on I Thess. iv, he retains
the formula 'called to be holy', and in I Cor. v and vi he refers
to a formula which he taught the Corinthians not many
months after his work in Thessalonica, according to which
those who commit the sins of uncleanness 'will not inherit the
Kingdom of God'[2] (vi, 10: compare Rev. xxi, 8). This does
not read like a phrase originated by St Paul. It is prefaced by
an allusion to 'defrauding the brethren'[3] (vi, 8), as in I Thess.
iv; it goes on to mention baptism (vi, 11); and it concludes
with a reference to the Holy Spirit (as in I Thessalonians,
and the Western version of the formula of Acts xv) and the
Christian *ekklēsia* as a 'sanctuary' or temple of 'the Spirit',
that is a neo-levitical system. (The idea is more fully
developed in I Peter ii.)

12. The actual list of sins consists of four in I Cor. v, 10,
six in v, 11, and ten in vi, 9 f.; but the basis of the lists might
be a triad, 'fornicator, covetous, idolater'. This triad reappears
in a new form in Eph. v, 3,[4] 'fornication, uncleanness,
covetousness which is idolatry', which is enlarged to a pentad
in Col. iii, 5 by the addition of 'passion' and 'evil lust',[5] a

1 Lev. xxiv, 19 says, 'As you did to another, so shall it be done to you',
which naturally gives birth to the negative counsel, 'Don't do to another
as you do not wish him to do to you.' This is the form found in *Two Ways*,
Aristides and the D text of Acts; Hillel and Tobit only vary by expressing
the subordinate clause as 'what you hate'. The maxim, in either case, is
a logical deduction from the *lex talionis*.

2 The phrase also occurs in Gal. v, 21 and Eph. v, 5. St Paul seldom
uses the phrase 'kingdom of God'; it does not seem to be part of his
normal vocabulary.

3 ἀδικεῖτε: I Thessalonians has ὑπερβαίνειν. πρᾶγμα is used in a peculiar
sense in both: I Cor. vi, 1 and I Thess. iv, 6.

4 With the reference to the 'kingdom of (Christ in) God'.

5 πάθος, ἐπιθυμία. It is clear that ἐπιθυμία (lust, desire) corresponds
in these documents to the Hebrew *yetser*, the 'evil inclination' inborn in
man. In *Mandata* there can be no question of this; for we find both the
good and evil ἐπιθυμία at war in the soul.

phrase which has a separate history, but occurs in all the forms of the apostolic tradition. 'Uncleanness' (*akatharsia*) in levitical thought would cover eating the blood; it is used as the antithesis of 'sanctification' in I Thess. iv, 7.

TABLE I. *The Holiness Code:* outline of passages from Lev. xvii–xx which are addressed to the people.

1. *The Uncleanness of Blood.* Lev. xvii.

   xvii, 1–9. The blood is to be poured on the altar.

   10–14. Not to eat the blood.

   15–16. The rite of Tebilah (immersion or baptism).

   Note: (1) These laws are incumbent on the *gēr* (alien, proselyte).

   (2) The Tebilah is probably the origin of proselyte baptism.

2. *Fornication.* Lev. xviii.

   xviii, 1–5. To keep the judgments, etc.
   Not to 'walk' like the Canaanites.

   6–23. Laws of affinity (fornication).

   24–30. Not to defile yourselves like the 'nations' (gentiles).

3. *A General Code of* Tōrāh. Lev. xix–xx. A basic catechism of elementary religious duties.

Note especially:	Matt.	I Thess.	I Pet.	I John	
xix, 2. 'Ye shall be holy: for I...your God am holy'	v, 48	iv, 7	i, 16	iii, 3	Consecration.
xix, 18. 'Thou shalt love thy neighbour as thyself'	v, 43	iv, 9	i, 22	iii, 10	Brotherly love.

   xx, 9–21. Penalties for fornication.

   22–26. Concluding exhortation.

   23. Not to 'walk' according to the manner of the 'gentiles'.

   26. Ye shall be holy.

Formulae of Introduction and Conclusion

In Christian literature we frequently find general formulae echoing levitical phrases such as are quoted above: 'not to walk', 'as the gentiles', etc. E.g. Eph. iv, 17: 'Not to walk as the gentiles walk in the vanity of their mind...through the ignorance that is in them...given themselves over to uncleanness, to work all wantonness in covetousness': where we find the three sins of uncleanness and also a specialised use of the word 'vanity' ($\mu\alpha\tau\alpha\iota\acute{o}\tau\eta\varsigma$) which, like 'falsehood' ($\psi\epsilon\hat{v}\delta\varsigma$), represent Hebrew words used for idols or idolatry.

See I Thess. iv, 5, Table II, next page.

PROSELYTE BAPTISM

TABLE II. *A Christian Holiness Code:* traces of neo-levitical requirements and formulae in the New Testament.

1. *The Prohibition of Blood* is included in the taboos of Acts xv, 29.

The Three Taboos or Sins of Uncleanness.

Acts xv, 29	I Cor. v, 11, etc.	Eph. v, 5 (cf. Col. iii, 5, Gal. v, 20)
Idolatry Fornication Blood	Fornicator Covetous Idolater	Fornication Uncleanness Covetousness which is Idolatry

2. *Neo-levitical* Tōrāh *in I Thessalonians, etc.*

I Thess. iv		I Pet. i	I John
1. How to walk...		Cf. 16	
3. your consecration, to 're-frain from fornication'	Acts xv, 29, I Cor. v, 9		
5. *not* in passion of *lust* as the gentiles...	Cf. Rom. xiii, 8 ff., as in Lev. xviii, etc.	14. *not*...the former *lusts* in the time of your ignorance	
6. not to overreach... in the 'business' his brother...	Cf. I Cor. vi, 8 Cf. I Cor. vi, 1 Cf. I Cor. vi, 8		
7. God did not *call* us in uncleanness, but in *consecration*...		15. Who *called* you to be holy: 'Be ye holy', **Lev. xix, 2** in all 'walking'	iii, 3
8. giving his Holy Spirit to us...		22. *Consecrating* your souls	
9. *brotherly love* to *love one another*...	Rom. xiii, 10, **Lev. xix, 18**	unto *brotherly love*... *Love one another*	iii, 10 iii, 11
11. to be quiet, mind one's own affairs, work with your hands...			
12. walk honestly with regard to those who are without	Rom. xiii, 13 Cf. I Cor. v, 12		
	Cf. I Cor. vi, 19	ii, 5. a spiritual temple	

It will be seen that I Thess. iv, 1–5 suggests the phraseology of Lev. xviii. The words 'passion' and 'lust', πάθος and ἐπιθυμία, are additions common in catechetical formulae, and represent the rabbinic *yetser*, or evil inclination; in Col. iii, 5 they are combined with the three sins of uncleanness.

Verses 7–9 echo the two great verses of Lev. xix. Lev. xix, 2 is actually quoted in I Pet. i, 16, which is another recension of the Thessalonian *tōrāh*; Rom. xiii, 10 comes from still another recension, and quotes Lev. xix, 18. The close relation between I Thess. iv–v, I Pet. i–ii, and Rom. xii–xiii is obvious to all students. Further parallels are exhibited in Table III.

The Christian community is compared to a sanctuary of the levitical type in I Corinthians as well as I Peter. In I Corinthians, St Paul is referring to teaching given in the Thessalonian period.

⟨ 19 ⟩

2-2

TABLE III.

I Thess. iv and v	Rom. xiii	Gal. v	I Pet. ii. Social Code
iv, 1. πᾶς...περιπατεῖν 3. *Your Sanctification* I Pet. i, 16, Lev. xix, 2	1. Let every soul be in subjection *Social Code*	13. ἐπ' ἐλευθερίᾳ... μὴ τὴν ἐλευθερίαν εἰς ἀφορμὴν σαρκί ἀλλὰ δουλεύετε ἀλλήλοις...	16. ὡς ἐλεύθεροι καὶ μὴ ὡς ἐπικάλυμμα... τὴν ἐλευθερίαν, ἀλλ' ὡς θεοῦ δοῦλοι...
9. τὸ ἀγαπᾶν ἀλλήλους I Pet. i, 22, Lev. xix, 18	9. ἀγαπήσεις τὸν πλησίον Quoting Lev. xix, 18	14. ἀγαπήσεις τὸν πλησίον Quoting Lev. xix, 18	17. τὴν ἀδελφότητα ἀγαπᾶτε
12. περιπατῆτε εὐσχημόνως	13. εὐσχημόνως περιπατήσωμεν 14. σαρκός...ἐπιθυμίας	16. πνεύματι περιπατεῖτε ἐπιθυμίαν σαρκός	12. ἀναστροφὴν...καλὴν See Jas. iii, 13 11. τῶν σαρκικῶν ἐπιθυμιῶν See Jas. iv, 1, Rom. vii, 23
v, 4f. ἡμέρα...νύξ 5. υἱοὶ φωτός οὐκ ἐσμὲν σκότους 8. θώρακα κ.τ.λ. 7. νυκτὸς μεθύουσιν 8. ἐνδυσάμενοι	12. ἡμέρα...νύξ ἔργα τοῦ σκότους ὅπλα τοῦ φωτός 13. μὴ κώμοις...μέθαις 14. ἐνδύσασθε	19. ἔργα τῆς σαρκός 20. πορνεία, ἀκαθαρσία... εἰδωλολατρεία... μέθαι κῶμοι	*Note.* These extracts are taken from I Pet. ii, 11–iii, 12, the second section in the epistle, dealing with social order, and partly identical with Rom. xii–xiii and I Thess. v. The first section has already been compared with I Thess. iv, and deals with the neo-levitical community.

This table is given (a) to make clear that our four authorities do actually represent the same thought sequence, though none except perhaps Peter gives more than part of it. All quote Lev. xix, 18, two quoting explicitly. The preceding verses in Peter and Galatians correspond: the succeeding verses in Galatians and Romans correspond; the next verses in Romans and Thessalonians closely correspond. Romans and Peter have at an earlier point (Rom. xiii, 1 ff., I Pet. ii, 13 ff.) versions of the same *tōrāh* about civil authority; this is preceded in Romans (ch. xii) and followed in Peter (after further social *tōrāh*) by moral teaching which has many points in common with each other, and with I Thessalonians; e.g. 'Pay back to no one evil for evil'; (b) to show the specifically Pauline dualism (light-darkness, flesh-spirit) which leads up to the command to clothe oneself with the armour of light; (c) to connect the teaching on 'brotherly love' or 'loving one another' with Lev. xix, 18 in each document, if all represent one thought sequence.

13. The inference is that St Paul is working from an early form of Christian *tōrāh* which involves three points:

(1) A taboo on certain unclean sins of a gentile character with a tendency to summarise them in a threefold formula (cf. Lev. xvii, 18).

(2) Baptism and reception of the Holy Spirit.

(3) Consecration as holy men in a holy community of which the leading character is love of the brethren (cf. Lev. xix).

The whole suggests a free development from Lev. xviiff.

The conclusion is of very great importance, because it means that in the earliest period of mission preaching Christianity was presented to the gentiles as a neo-levitical community. Outside was the dark gentile world whose unclean practices were renounced; baptism cleansed its recipient from defilement (the word *hamartia*, sin, is never free from this conception) and was the occasion on which he received the Holy Spirit. This was not, however, an individual or subjective experience; it was, rather, the incorporation or adoption of the convert into the community in which the Holy Spirit lived, the brotherhood which was the sanctuary of God himself, whose spirit consecrated it in love. The divine community of Leviticus is the pattern and progenitor of the new.

St Peter prefers the word 'brotherhood' for the community; St James calls it a 'synagogue'; but the common word is that of St Paul or St John, *ekklēsia*, which is translated 'church'.

SUMMARY OF CHAPTER III

It has often been assumed that certain passages in I Peter which resemble passages in the Pauline writings are in fact derived from those writings. It is more likely that both writers are using the same formulae which are older than either documents.

A comparison of the warning in I Pet. i, 6, Rom. v, 4, and Jas. i, 2 confirms this supposition. A similar warning is found in the opening sentences of the Jewish proselyte baptism ritual, Ecclesiasticus, the *Two Ways, Mandata,* and the Sermon on the Mount. Jewish catechetical material may as a rule have opened with a reference to temptation, affliction, or persecution, and also have added to the initial virtue of faith the virtues of hope and endurance. Christian teaching seems to have added love to hope-endurance, and joy to temptation (affliction).

I Thessalonians exhibits these opening formulae.

I Peter is nearer in general outline to James than to any Pauline writing; yet differences in vocabulary and general tone are so great as to preclude the explanation that one borrowed from the other. Both exhibit a succession of thought and terminology which is best thought of as prior to either.

CHAPTER III

I PETER AND PARALLELS

1. The suggestion of Perdelwitz[1] that I Peter (which I shall henceforth designate as Peter) contains an exhortation to candidates for baptism has met with favourable reception by scholars,[2] and sheds light on the epistle, enabling us to formulate some answer to the question, 'By whom, to whom, and under what circumstances were these words spoken?' It is also in harmony with the general tendency to regard much of the New Testament literature as a transcript of catechetical material which may in some cases be of Jewish origin. Further, it relieves us of the necessity of supposing that some of Peter is to be explained as a literary borrowing from Paul; for the similarities are such as to suggest a different and more remote type of contact. We should look rather for two allied communities whose oral *tōrāh* has a common ancestry.

Joy in Temptation (Affliction)

2. Let us take an example:

Pet. i, 6	Rom. v, 3
Ye rejoice,	We boast
though grieved for a little if need be,	in our afflictions, knowing that
through various temptations,	affliction works patience,
that the *testing* of your faith...	and patience *testing*,
might be found unto honour and praise and glory...	and testing hope

It is scarcely possible to regard the Petrine passage as a

1 R. Perdelwitz, *Die Mysterienreligionen und das Problem des I Petrusbriefes*. It is unfortunate that this writer should have been drawn away from recognising the Hebrew traditions in Peter by the lure of the 'mystery religions'.
2 Notably B. H. Streeter in *The Primitive Church*. See also J. C. Wand on I Peter in the Westminster series.

literary derivation from the Pauline, as the vocabulary is so different; besides, the words 'knowing that' in Romans seem to introduce a well-known saying, so that, if there were any dependence, the probability would be that St Paul borrows from St Peter. A closer parallel is found in James:

Pet. i, 6	Jas. i, 2
Ye *rejoice* though grieved for a little if need be, through *various temptations*, that *the testing of your faith*... might be found unto honour and praise and glory.	Count it all *joy*, my brethren, when ye fall into *various temptations*, knowing that, *the testing of your faith* worketh patience.

3. We note that in James, too, the aphorism is introduced, as a quotation, and, while the 'various temptations' and the 'testing of your faith' agree verbally with Peter, the 'worketh patience' agrees verbally with Romans; the word 'hope' (*elpis*) which is present in Romans is absent from the whole epistle of James, and the word 'patience' or 'endurance' (*hupomonē*) which is common to Romans and James is absent from the whole epistle of Peter. We are dealing with radically different uses of language. *Elpis* and *hupomonē* are homonyms, which may both represent the Hebrew word *mikweh*; one is used in the school of Peter, and the other in the school of James. Dr Gavin points out that *mikweh* also means a 'congregation of waters' suitable for baptism, and that R. Akiba in a celebrated pun on this word connected hope with baptism (Yomah viii, 9).

4. We note that in Peter and James the formula is part of the opening of the epistle; and an agreement in order adds much to the force of a mere verbal agreement. In Jewish proselyte baptism [1] also the first step was to warn the candidate

---

[1] The references to the Jewish baptismal rite are taken by F. L. Gavin from the tractates Yebamoth and Gerim, which, though later in date than the New Testament, are not likely to have been influenced by Christian thought or practice.

that he must expect afflictions and persecutions; but a much earlier and closer parallel is to be found in Ecclus. ii, 1 (the first word addressed to the learner personally), 'My son, if thou approachest to serve the Lord, prepare thy soul for temptation', which goes on like Peter (but not James) to the metaphor of testing gold in the furnace. Indeed Ecclus. i–ii is a rich storehouse of New Testament vocabulary, demanding as it does meekness, humility, and other child-like qualities of the learner; it gives us one version of the usual opening formulae of the Jewish school of *tōrāh*, of which other examples may be studied in the *Two Ways*, the *Mandata*, and the Matthaean version of the Sermon on the Mount; for the Beatitudes, like James-Peter, lay emphasis on rejoicing in persecution.

Faith-Hope-Endurance

5. Ecclus. ii, 7–9 affords a triad of virtues which are demanded at the beginning from the learner: endurance, faith, and hope. The first 'commandment' of Hermas is faith, and in James the same initial virtue is assumed. Hope-endurance (or patience) is the next stage; and the familiar Christian triad is formed by adding love; but the faith-hope-endurance triad is the original concept, and love is an addition to it. This distinction is preserved in the New Testament and subapostolic writers, especially by St John and St Ignatius who speak of faith and love as the fundamental 'commandments'.[1] Faith has to do with baptism in the New Testament, and hope seems to be connected with it; *episteusa* practically means 'I was baptised'. Love has to do with the eucharist (or *agapē*) and life in the holy brotherhood. Faith-hope-love is

[1] In the gospel and epistles of St John, there is a characteristic use of the word 'commandment', e.g. John xiii, 34, I John, ii, 7. The 'commandment' is 'new', yet not new, because his hearers had heard it from the beginning (i.e. at their baptismal instruction?). It is twofold, faith and love: 'This is his commandment, that we should *believe on the name* of his Son Jesus Christ, and *love one another*, as he gave us commandment' (I John, iii, 23).

a phrase which sums up the whole Christian life; faith-love is shorter yet.

6. It is best, therefore, to think that our various authorities are transcripts of different forms of the same piece of *tōrāh*, a formula with which Jewish catechisms commonly opened; but the close resemblances among the Christian authorities permit us to ask whether it is possible to think that there was a Christian *tōrāh* already settled prior to the date of the apostolic writings. St Paul alludes to such *tōrāh* in I Thessalonians,[1] makes use in the first sentence of that epistle of the faith-hope-love formula (I Thess. i, 3), and speaks only a line or two later (I Thess. i, 6) of rejoicing in temptations and persecutions.

The Inner Warfare

7. Another example of a common formula is found in a phrase connected with the familiar Jewish concept of a dramatic psychological dualism. Pet. ii, 11 speaks of the 'fleshly lusts which make war (*strateuontai*) against the soul', which is parallel to Jas. iv, 1, 'your delights which make war (*strateuontai*) in your members'. It is true that the word in James is *hēdonai* (delights) not *epithumiai* as in Peter; but the next word is *epithumeite* (ye lust).

8. The parallel passage in Paul is found in Rom. vii, 23, 'I perceive another law in my members making war against (*antistrateuomenon*) the law of my mind'. This parallel has been used to show that Peter is dependent on Paul; but the more likely inference is that all three authors are echoing what is a commonplace in catechetical teaching; and we note that, as in the former case, James and Peter are more like one another than either is like Paul. Another form of the same concept is found in Gal. v, 17, 'the flesh lusteth against the spirit'. The original idea is that of the soul as a gift received from

1 I Thess. i, 3 and v, 8. It is also found in Heb. x, 22 ff., where it is followed by a reference to endurance; Heb. xi deals with faith as a kind of hope or endurance. It would be difficult to prove that these passages owed anything to the Pauline writings.

God in a pure and holy condition,[1] to be preserved against all contamination.[2]

9. The similarity of diction between the texts we have quoted may not seem to be very striking; but it is taken as one example of the many similarities which have led scholars to assume that there is some relationship between the documents in which they occur.

Wisdom

10. Returning to the opening phrases of our documents, we may now make a negative point. In Jas. i, 5 the learners are told to pray for wisdom; and St Paul actually opens his epistles with such a prayer, which no doubt reflects the usage of his school. It is curious that this point is missing at the opening of Peter.[3]

Peter and James

11. Peter exhibits many more parallels with James than with any epistle of St Paul. But before exhibiting the parallels it is necessary to allude to the theory, endorsed by Jülicher, that Peter consists of two epistles,[4] the break occurring between iv, 11 and 12. The justification for

---

1 Lack of space forbids us to develop the Jewish doctrine of the soul, for which see G. F. Moore, *Judaism*. Man's soul (*nephesh*) is a breath from God which is lent him for his lifetime, and returned at death; it must not be contaminated by evil. E.g. Lev. xx, 25, 'ye shall not make your *nephesh* abominable' by eating impure meats. In *Zadokite Fragment*, viii, 20, this phrase has already become, 'man shall not make abominable his holy spirit'; with which compare Test. Nap. (Hebrew) x, 9, 'Blessed is the man who does not defile his holy spirit of God'. In Eph. iv, 30, we read, 'grieve not the Holy Spirit of God', where this type of thought has been given a Christian turn; but the original idea survives in Mand. x, 5.

2 'Saving the soul' is, therefore, preserving it pure and holy from contamination by the evil inclination (*yetser*, ἐπιθυμία) which makes war against it.

3 It is found, of course, at the beginning of Proverbs, Ecclesiasticus, etc. St Paul's prayer is that converts should grow and come to maturity, with regard to such rabbinic virtues as 'knowledge', 'wisdom', and 'understanding' (Col. i, 9, etc.).

4 The arguments for dividing I Peter are not decisive. The theory is assumed throughout this book, because it does correspond to a certain duplication in the evidence which is adduced.

accepting some such division will appear in the next chapter; but, if we assume it for the present, it will be seen that there are a great number of similarities between Peter and James, and that, for the most part, they occur in the same order; that is to say, the references under Peter A and Peter B are practically in correct succession. The chances against such a coincidence are, of course, very great; and the best explanation, indeed the only one which occurs to me, is that both are reproducing the same system of oral teaching, which was so given that one formula tended to bring up the next one in the mind by association. The parallelism only extends over James i, 1–iv, 10.

Parallel Passages in Peter and James

James		Peter A	Peter B
i, 1	The Diaspora	i, 1	
i, 2	Various temptations	i, 6	
i, 3	Testing of faith	i, 7	
i, 11	Isa. xl, 6	i, 24	
i, 12	The crown		v, 4
i, 18	Begotten by a word	i, 23	
i, 21	Salvation	ii, 2 (i, 9)	
i, 27	Pure worship (spiritual sacrifice)	ii, 5	
iii, 13	Honest 'walking'	ii, 12	
iv, 1	Lusts making war	ii, 11	
iv, 6	Prov. iii, 34		v, 5b
iv, 7	Submit		v, 5a
iv, 7	Resist the devil		v, 9
iv, 10	Be humbled		v, 6

12. While this thought sequence runs through both epistles, it has been so differently coloured in each as to produce a totally different effect. In James we are in a rabbinic school of the type of Ecclesiasticus, transfigured by the *tōrāh* of the Sermon on the Mount; in Peter we have the sacred community of Leviticus, with some features of the passover meal,[1] and

1 Paschal formulae in I Peter: sprinkling of blood, i, 2; girding up the loins, i, 13 (used only once elsewhere in the New Testament, Luke xii, 35, where the imagery is that of a meal); lamb without blemish, i, 19. These are redemption formulae like those in *Mekilta*; formulae based on Lev. xix may be called consecration formulae.

Christ presented as the paschal lamb. It is impossible to suppose that either author could have performed the literary feat of extracting the thought sequence from the other, and then giving it so new an expression. The difference is more simply explained as the natural divergence of two living organisms derived from one stock, but developing separately.

13. The parallels between Peter and the Pauline epistles are more subtle, and extend over I Thessalonians, Romans, Ephesians (Colossians) and even Galatians. An attempt will be made in the next chapter to trace a sequence in these parallels.

SUMMARY OF CHAPTER IV

We proceed to a study of material common to Colossians, Ephesians, I Peter, and James.

Four phrases are chosen for study which occur (with only slight variation or omission) in the same order in all four. As some of them occur twice in Peter, that epistle is divided at iv, 11/12 into two parts, Peter A and B.

The phrases are

    (1) Wherefore putting off all evil... (*Deponentes*),
    (2) Submit yourselves... (*Subiecti*),
    (3) Watch and pray... (*Vigilate*),
    (4) Resist the devil... (*Resistite*),

each one, it is suggested, being characteristic of, and therefore serving to name, a whole section.

Extended outline of Sections

    (1) Being begotten again by the word, *or*
        the new man being created in you,
        Put off all evil... (and falsehood)
        exercise the virtues of a catechumen,
        offer worship to God and the Father.
    (2) Submit yourselves to the elders (*or* to God).
    (3) Watch and pray.
    (4) Resist the devil (*or* stand firm).

'Tabloid' form in I Cor. xvi, 13 f.
Traces in Hebrews.

CHAPTER IV

THE FOUR POINTS

1. The resemblances between Ephesians, I Peter and James have long been noted, but have usually been attributed to the literary influence of the Pauline epistles on later writers; there is, however, another method of research. It may be possible by a synoptic comparison to discover a common source for the passages common to all three, or more probably a common pattern according to which all three developed. On attempting this task it was found necessary to include Colossians in the survey; and thus five documents are employed, counting Peter as two, for the pattern which is discovered occurs almost twice in Peter.[1] It is also faintly preserved in Hebrews.

2. Neglecting the formulae which have already been dealt with, and concentrating on the more obvious similarities, we are left with four phrases which occur with but little variation of diction or order in all four epistles. As they are initial words, we may also use them to denote the sections which they introduce, using the Latin tongue in order to avoid confusion. They are:

(1) *Deponentes igitur omne malum.*   (2) *Subiecti estote.*
(3) *Vigilate (et Orate).*   (4) *Resistite diabolo* (or *State*).

TABLE IV.

	Col.	Eph.	Pet. A	Pet. B	Jas.	Heb.
Deponentes	iii, 8	iv, 25	ii, 1	—	i, 21	xii, 1
Subiecti	iii, 18	v, 21	ii, 13	v, 5	iv, 7	xii, 9
Vigilate	iv, 2	*vi, 18	*iv, 7	v, 8	—	*xiii, 17
Resistite	(iv, 12)	vi, 11	—	v, 9	iv, 7	—

Note:

(1) * signifies a variation in the Greek word employed.

(2) Round brackets signify a phrase which may be regarded as a substitute.

(3) Peter is divided in order to exhibit the partial duplication of the evidence.

---

[1] I Peter is alluded to as Peter. I Pet. i, 1–iv, 11 is called Peter A; I Peter iv, 12 to end is called Peter B. In quoting James, I refer only to Jas. i, 1–iv, 12, as the remainder of this epistle is of a different character.

PRIMITIVE CHRISTIAN CATECHISM

Putting off all Evil

3. *Deponentes Igitur.* The epistles of the New Testament may as a rule be divided into two parts (*a*) expository, (*b*) an exhortation to piety. In Ephesians and Colossians we find early in the latter part an introductory formula containing the verb *apotithesthai* (to put off). Omitting five verses in Ephesians which have no parallel in Colossians, we have:

Eph. iv, 25 and 31	Col. ii, 8, 9
Wherefore *putting off* lying speak truth... *all* bitterness and wrath and anger and clamour and blasphemy be removed from you with all *evil*	And now *put off* also *all* anger, wrath, *evil* blasphemy, shameful speaking out of your mouth. Lie not to one another

The parallels in Peter and James occur nearer the beginning of the document:

Pet. ii, 1, 2	Jas. i, 21
Putting off therefore all evil and all guile and hypocrisies and envies and all contradictions, As new-born babes, ye longed for the guileless milk of the *word*, that in it ye may grow into *salvation.*	*Wherefore putting off all* filth, and excess of *evil,* receive in meekness the implanted *word* which is able to *save* your souls.

These formulae are clearly versions of one formula, which is distinct from the call to renounce gentile sins of uncleanness,[1] and also from the common caution about the *epithumia*, or evil desire, which occurs in all our documents.

(*a*) In each case (except James) there are five sins enumerated;[2] and they are on the whole sins of speech.

(*b*) In each case the word *kakia* occurs (evil, viciousness, malice). All except James mention deceit or lying.

---

1 In Ephesians and Colossians the renunciation of gentile sins of uncleanness is associated with the *Deponentes*, preceding it in Colossians, following it in Ephesians. The renunciation of the evil inclination, ἐπιθυμία, is combined with it in Colossians in such a way as to turn the triad into a pentad.

2 In Colossians the literary scheme seems to be built on the figure five. There are five sins of uncleanness instead of three; and there are five sins of speech under the *Deponentes* succeeded by five virtues.

(c) In Peter the converts next 'desire the milk of the word': in James they 'receive the word'. In Paul, however, we find the command to 'put on', a logical antithesis to the original counsel to 'put off', but nevertheless peculiar to Paul.

(d) Nor are we at the end of our comparison. In three of the four cases the formula 'putting off all evil' has a 'therefore' in front of it, which links it with a preceding paragraph.[1] In Ephesians the preceding paragraph refers to the 'new man' who is 'created' or 'renewed' in the believer 'according to the image of the creator'; in James and Peter it refers to a 'birth' or 'rebirth by a word'; they represent two independent but closely related modes of referring to the great change of status and condition which occurs in connection with baptism; in James the noun *ktisma* (creation) actually occurs in the birth formula in reference to the thing born.

4. If we compare Ephesians and Colossians, we find our comparison impeded by the interpolation of definitely Pauline formulae, that is to say, formulae which seem characteristic of St Paul himself, and have no parallel in James and Peter. The extraneous character of this material is shown by the fact that the order in which it is interpolated is different in Ephesians and Colossians. If we confine our attention to formulae which are found in both epistles in the same order,[2] neglecting passages found only in one epistle, or passages found in both but inserted at very different points, we are left with the table of parallels (on page 34) which gives us a common groundwork.

5. In this table the bracketed passages need not be considered as they contain material peculiar to one epistle only. We may also neglect the passage on fornication and other sins of uncleanness (Col. iii, 5 = Eph. v, 3), which, as we have already seen (Chapter II), belongs to the neo-levitical catechism for gentile proselytes. Another passage which may not

1 The word 'therefore' is lacking in Colossians because the *Deponentes* precedes the new-birth formula.

2 With the exception of Eph. iv, 1–4 which seems to be preserved in its true place in Col. iii, 12–15.

PRIMITIVE CHRISTIAN CATECHISM

be original in this context is the formula of the old man and
the new man which is characteristic of St Paul, and, like the
sins of uncleanness, is found at a different point in each

<table>
<tr><td colspan="2">Colossians</td><td>Ephesians</td></tr>
<tr><td></td><td></td><td>iv, 1. ...to walk worthily... (A 2)</td></tr>
<tr><td></td><td></td><td>2. with all lowliness and meekness (C 4),</td></tr>
<tr><td></td><td></td><td>3. with long-suffering (C 4), forbearing one another... (C 5) in the bond of peace; (C 9, 10)</td></tr>
<tr><td></td><td></td><td>4. one body...ye were called... (C 11)</td></tr>
<tr><td></td><td></td><td>(5–16. Unity of the church. 17–20. Not to walk like gentiles.)</td></tr>
<tr><td>A 1
2
3</td><td>ii, 6. As ye received Christ...
walk in him...
as ye were taught...
(8–19. False teachers.
20–iii, 4. Dying with Christ.)
iii, 5. Fornication, uncleanness...idolatry.</td><td>20. You did not so learn Christ...
were taught in him...
22. To put off the old man...
24. To put on the new man...
Created according to God...</td></tr>
<tr><td>B 1
2
3</td><td>8. And now put off also all anger, wrath,
evil, blasphemy, shameful speaking, out
of your mouth, lie not to one another...
9. Stripping off the old man...
10. Putting on the new...
Renewed...according to the...
Creator.
(11. Neither Greek nor Jew.=Gal. iii, 28.)</td><td>25. Wherefore putting off lying, speak
truth each with his neighbour,...
29. every evil word out of your
mouth...
31. all bitterness, and wrath, and
anger, and outcry, and blas-
phemy...
...with all evil.

(Verses omitted peculiar to Ephesians.)</td></tr>
<tr><td>C 1
2
3
4
5
6
7
8
9
10
11
12</td><td>12. Put on, as men chosen of God,
holy and beloved,
bowels of mercy, kindness,
lowliness, meekness, long-suffering;
13. forbearing one another
and forgiving one another...
as also the Lord forgave you...
14. Above all this, love
which is the bond of perfection.
15. and the peace of Christ...
ye were called in one body;
and be thankful.
16. (The word of Christ dwell in you richly in all wisdom.)</td><td>32. And become to one another

kind and merciful,

forgiving one another,
as also God in Christ
forgave you...
v, 1. as beloved children.
And walk in love.
3. Fornication, uncleanness, etc.

(Verses omitted characteristic of Ephesians.)</td></tr>
</table>

epistle; it will be noted that its presence creates a doublet in
each document for the *Deponentes*. On the other hand, the
material in Eph. iv, 1–4 looks as if it were found in its proper
context in Col. iii, 12–15, and had been differently placed in
Ephesians (*a*) to allow the catechumen virtues to open the

paraenetic part of the epistle, and (*b*) to provide a good opening
('in one body') for the passage on the unity of the church.[1]

6. The resultant Pauline *Deponentes* opens with a reference
to teaching which has been received, goes on to urge the
putting off of sins of speech, and inculcates three types of
virtue, (*a*) truth-telling, (*b*) catechumen virtues of meekness,
and (*c*) love, which follow from the possession of a new
status 'as men chosen of God, holy and beloved', or 'as
beloved children'. Only in Col. iii, 16 is there a reference to
the 'word' as in James and Peter.

7. The parallels in James and Peter are easier to set out:

Peter	James
i, 22. Consecrating your souls in the obedience of *truth*...	(i, 10 f. Quotes Isa. xl, 6)
23. being *begotten* again, not of corruptible seed but uncorruptible, by a *word* of God living and abiding;	i, 18. by an act of will he *begat* us
(24. Quotes Isa. xl, 6)	by a *word* of *truth* that we should be a kind of firstfruits
25. and this is the word evangelised unto you.	of his creations...
ii, 1. *Wherefore putting off all evil* and all guile, etc.,	19, 20. ...be swift to hear, etc.
2. as newborn infants desire the guileless milk of *the word*, that by it you may grow unto *salvation*...	21. *Wherefore putting off all* filth and excess of *evil*, in meekness receive *the* implanted *word* which can *save* your souls.
	22. Be doers of the word.

We see by this comparison that the *Deponentes* in James and
Peter also urges the catechumen virtues in view of the new
status which has been achieved; but these writers speak of a
'new birth' by a 'word', whereas St Paul prefers the thought

1 Col. iii, 12–15 reads like a literary unity; it is not easy to suppose that
it was created by combining the two passages from Ephesians. 'Forbearing
one another and forgiving one another', for instance, sounds like an
original parallelism. The whole passage in Colossians is homogeneous,
Jewish in tone, and less broken than the corresponding passages in
Ephesians. See p. 60.

of the creation of a new man. James and Peter use at this point a formula for the Christian message which St Paul places at the beginning of the first part of Ephesians and Colossians.

Colossians	Ephesians
i, 5. Ye *heard* beforehand in the *word* of the *gospel*...	i, 13. *hearing* the *word* of truth
6. bearing fruit and growing... in truth	the *gospel* of your *salvation*

The Christian message, or 'word', is here, as in James and Peter, a vitalising 'truth', with a 'saving' power. In Peter it is seed; in James it is implanted; in Colossians it grows and bears fruit.

8. I believe that these facts are sufficient to justify us in stating that the phrase *Deponentes* comes at the same point in each of the four epistles; that is, it occupies the same position in a similar thought sequence, a point at which the status of the believer is defined as a new birth or a new creation. This conclusion is confirmed by what immediately follows:

Colossians	Ephesians
iii, 15. be thankful.	
16. The word of Christ dwell richly in you in all wisdom.	v, 18. Be filled with the Spirit,
Teaching and admonishing *one another*	19. speaking to *one another*
in psalms, hymns, spiritual songs...	*in psalms* and *hymns* and *spiritual songs,*
singing in your hearts to God	*singing* and making melody *in your hearts*
17. and all you do, in word or in deed, *all in the name of* the *Lord Jesus,*	to the Lord,
giving thanks to God the Father	*giving thanks* always for *all in the name of our Lord Jesus* Christ
through him.	*to God* and *the Father.*

⟨ 36 ⟩

We find here that the indwelling of the word (in Colossians), or of the Spirit (in Ephesians), is followed by a solemn worship addressed to God (and) the Father. The picture of a spirit-filled community indwelt by a divine power (cf. I Cor. iii, 16 and II Cor. vi, 16 = Lev. xxvi, 11) is ultimately based on sanctuary symbolism; those who offer the spiritual worship are the 'elect' and 'holy' of Col. iii, 12, or the 'beloved children' of Eph. v, 1, who are entitled by their new birth (or creation) to invoke God as Father (Pet. i, 17).

9. St Peter goes on to describe this holy community in levitical language (ii, 4–10), speaking of a 'spiritual temple' and a 'holy priesthood' offering 'spiritual sacrifices acceptable to God through Jesus Christ' (Pet. ii, 5). St James, when he has finished with the catechumen virtues, refers in language derived from the levitical cultus to a 'pure worship and undefiled before God and the Father' (Jas. i, 27). The *Deponentes*, then, would appear to have a secure place in a thought sequence common to all four documents.

The Code of Subordination[1]

10. The next keyword common to all four documents is the *Subiecti Estote*. In Ephesians and Colossians we find immediately after the section just studied (the *Deponentes*) a 'code of subordination' to husbands, fathers, and masters of slaves, that is, to the elders of the community in the primitive sense of the term (Eph. v, 21 ff. = Col. iii, 18 ff.). A similar code is found at the same point in Peter A (ii, 13 ff.), though there is a fresh introduction (ii, 11–12) which resembles Jas. iv, 1 and iii, 13, and it is enriched with other material which closely resembles Rom. xii and xiii;[2] it ends with five social virtues similar to the five virtues which form part of the *Deponentes*

---

1 The phrase 'code of subordination', κανών τῆς ὑποτάξεως, is applied to this kind of catechetical teaching by St Clement (i, 3).

2 The doctrine of subordination to the elders is only part of a larger doctrine of subordination, which opens with the honour due to the king, and links it with the idea of the holy community in which mutual love and subordination reign. St Peter here makes a fresh beginning, and devotes a whole section to this subject.

in Colossians, 'of one mind, feeling for one another, loving the brethren, merciful, lowly-minded'.

11. In Peter B and James there is no such code; but the *Subiecti* introduces what are obviously versions of the same passage of teaching:

Peter B	James
v, 5. Likewise ye younger, *submit* to the elders; and all to one another. (Eph. v, 21) Be girded with humility. (Quotes *Prov. iii, 34*)	iv, 6. (Quotes *Prov. iii, 34*) 7. *Submit* then to God. *Resist the devil...*
6. *Humble yourselves* then, under the mighty hand of God, that *he* may *exalt you* in due season.	10. *Humble yourselves* before the Lord, and *he* shall *exalt you.*
8. *The devil...9...resist*	

In this manifest parallel we note the interesting divergence in the *Subiecti* clause between subordination to God (James) and to the elders (Peter). Eph. v, 21 agrees with Peter B in the additional phrase 'submit to one another'. We also note the associated word 'be humbled' introducing the familiar paradox of the exaltation of the humble, which is found seven times in the gospels, and is older than that (cf. Ecclus. i, 30). Peter A has a reference to 'humble-mindedness' at the end of his code of subordination; this word occurs in Colossians in the *Deponentes* (iii, 12), but in Ephesians it occurs much earlier (iv, 1).

12. Once again, surely, in spite of differences of handling we are justified in saying that the keyword *Subiecti Estote* introduces a similar passage in each of our sources, though Ephesians, Colossians, and Peter A suggest one mode of presentation, while Peter B and James suggest a different one. In the former case it succeeds the *Deponentes* very closely (though new introductory matter intervenes in Peter A); in the latter case it follows at a greater distance. In every

case except James it implies submission to the elders; and yet James is manifestly a version of the same exhortation as Peter B.

Watch (*and Pray*)

13. *Vigilate.* Three of our major authorities agree in a reference both to watching and praying. In Colossians it comes immediately after the last section we have studied (the *Subiecti*). In Peter A there is intervening material, some of which has echoes in Ephesians, but not Colossians. In Ephesians it follows the *Resistite*:

Eph. vi, 18. *Praying* at every season in the Spirit
and *watching* thereto in all perseverance.
Col. iv, 2. In *prayer* persevere,
watching thereto in thanksgiving.
Pet. iv, 7 (A). Be sober therefore
and *watch* unto *prayer.*

In each case the phrase occurs in the final exhortation (allowing that Peter is divisible); and in each case it introduces a reference to speaking the word.

Eph. vi, 19. For me, that a *word* (*logos*) may be given me.
Col. iv, 6. Your *word* (*logos*) ever in grace. .
Pet. iv, 11 (A). If any one speaks, as the *oracles* (*logia*) of God.

14. In our fourth major authority (James) the *Vigilate* is missing. Its place is taken by the words, 'Cleanse your hands ye sinners, and purify your hearts ye double-minded. Mourn and lament and weep' (iv, 8). But we do find it represented in Peter B (which so closely resembles James here as to be in most respects identical), though the reference to prayer is missing.

Pet. v, 8. Brethren, be sober, *watch.*

It immediately succeeds the *Subiecti*.

Resist the Devil (or *Stand Firm*)

15. *Resistite.* The reference to the devil at the end of Ephesians, Peter, and the first part of James has always been regarded as a striking similarity which calls for careful

consideration, all the more because nowhere else in the New Testament does the command to resist the devil occur. It does occur, however, in the *Testaments of the Twelve Patriarchs* and the *Mandata* of Hermas; and the command in James is verbally identical with that in the former.

> Jas. iv, 7. *Resist* the *devil* and he will flee from you.
> (Test. Nap. viii, 4, see also Mand. xii, 4–7.)

The *Resistite* is not found in Peter A, but occurs in Peter B in the passage which so closely resembles James.

> Pet. v, 8. Your adversary the *devil*...whom *resist*.

16. In Ephesians it forms part of the magnificent picture of the armed combat with evil, which has no parallel in the New Testament outside the Pauline writings (but see *Testaments* and *Mandata*). It is placed before the *Vigilate*. It is not found in Colossians; but its place is taken by the word 'stand'; 'that you may *stand* perfect' (iv, 12), which is connected with the 'prayer' and 'agonising' (prayer-combat) of Epaphras. This word also occurs in the final paragraph of Peter B (v, 12) and is used three times in the combat with the devil (*Resistite*) of Ephesians. See p. 86, n. 1.

> vi, 11. That you may be able to *stand* against the wiles of the devil...
> 13. that you may be able to *resist*...and to *stand*...
> 14. *stand* therefore

Colossians, therefore, does not entirely fail us.

The Four Phrases

17. The case may now be summarised as follows:

(1) *Deponentes Igitur*. All four documents.
(2) *Subiecti Estote*. All four documents: doubled in Peter.
(3) *Vigilate*. Three documents (not James): doubled in Peter.
(4) *Resistite*. Three documents (not Colossians, unless 'stand perfect' is admitted).
(*Note:* in Ephesians the *Resistite* precedes the *Vigilate*.)

The duplication of (2) and (3) in Peter may be explained by dividing the epistle, giving (1), (2), (3) to Peter A, and (2), (3), (4) to Peter B.[1] An interesting *prima facie* case has been made out; for (3) and (4) seem in reality to form a unity, and the actual impression given is as follows:

	Eph.	Col.	Peter A	Peter B	James
(2)	Be subject (iv, 2)	Be subject (iii, 12)	Be subject Humble-minded	Be subject Be humble	Be subject Be humble
(4)	Stand Resist	(3) Prayer Watching	Watch Prayer	Watch	—
(3)	Praying Watching	(4) Stand	—	Resist Stand	Resist

As we look at this synopsis, another example at once flashes into the mind, in which we are given something very like this tabloid form. As in the case of Peter B and James it serves to close an epistle; only, as there is no other paraenetic material, it seems to summarise it all.

> I Cor. xvi, 13. Watch,
> Stand firm in the faith,
> Play the man, be strong.
> 14. Let all your deeds be done in love...
> 16. Be subject...

Hebrews

18. The Epistle to the Hebrews shows traces of the same pattern:

(1) *Deponentes* xii, 1.
(2) *Subiecti* xii, 9. (Cf. xiii, 17.)
(3) *Vigilate* xiii, 17.

As is well known, this author does not intend to go over the elementary work of baptismal catechesis, which he compares,

---

1 It might therefore be supposed that Chapter iv had been omitted from Peter A, and Chapter i from Peter B, when the two documents were combined. It is perhaps more probable that the *Deponentes* was not required in Peter B, because this document is not baptismal in character, being an exhortation to martyrdom addressed primarily to the elders; the *Resistite*, being a strong formula of conclusion, is reserved to form a dramatic end to the whole document.

Colossians (iii, 8–iv, 12)	Ephesians (iv, 22–vi, 19)
i, 5. The word of the gospel... fruit-bearing and growing...in truth	i, 13. The word of truth... the gospel of your salvation
The New Creation iii, 9. [Putting off the old man... 10. Putting on the new, who is being renewed unto knowledge according to the image of him who created him]	**The New Creation** iv, 22. Put off the old man... 24. Put on the new man, who is created according to God in righteousness and holiness of the truth
Deponentes 8. And now put off also all wrath, anger, evil, blasphemy, shameful speaking, out of your mouth 9. Lie not to one another. (For 9b and 10 see above)	**Deponentes** 25. Wherefore, putting off lying, speak truth... 29. No bad word out of your mouth... 31. All bitterness, and anger, and wrath... with all evil
Catechumen Virtues **Worship of God** 16. The Word of Christ... In psalms, hymns, spiritual songs... 17. All in the Name of the Lord Jesus, giving thanks to God the Father through him	**Catechumen Virtues** **Worship of God** v, 18. In the Spirit... 19. In psalms, and hymns, and spiritual songs... 20. Giving thanks...in the Name of our Lord Jesus Christ to God and the Father
Subiecti 18. Wives be subject, etc.	**Subiecti** 21. Being subject to one another in the fear of Christ
Code of Subordination (to husbands, parents, masters of slaves, i.e. the elders) [humble-mindedness. Cf. iii, 12]	**Code of Subordination** (to husbands, parents, masters of slaves, i.e. the elders) [humble-mindedness. Cf. iv, 2]
Vigilate iv, 2. In prayer persevere, watching thereto in thanksgiving 3. Praying also at the same time for us that God may open to us the door of the word. (iv, 6. Your word)	**Vigilate** vi, 18. [In all prayer and supplication, praying at every season in the Spirit, and watching thereto... 19. And for me, that a word may be given me...]
Resistite (nil) **State** 12. Epaphras salutes you...always agonising for you in his prayers that you may stand perfect	**Resistite. State** 11. Put on the whole armour of God... to stand against the wiles of the devil 13. That you may be able to resist...and to stand 14. Stand therefore

V.

attention to a variation in order.

I Peter (Peter A, i, 1–iv, 11. Peter B, iv, 12–v, 14)		James (i, 1–iv, 10)
The New Birth		**The New Birth**
i, 22. In obedience of truth... 23. Being begotten again, not of corruptible seed, but of incorruptible, through a word of God, living and abiding... 25. And this is the word which was 'evangelised' unto you		i, 18. By an act of will he begat us with a living word, that we should be a kind of firstfruit of his creations... 19. Slow to anger...
Deponentes		**Deponentes**
ii, 1. Putting off, therefore, all evil, and all guile, and hypocrisies, and envies, and all contradictions 2. As new-born babes, long for the guileless milk of the word, that by it you may grow unto salvation		21. Wherefore putting off all filth and excess of evil, receive in meekness the implanted word which is able to save your souls
The Living Temple **Worship of God**		**Catechumen Virtues** **Worship of God**
5. Unto a holy priesthood, to offer spiritual sacrifices, acceptable to God, through Jesus Christ		27. Pure religious observance and undefiled before God and the Father...
Subiecti		**Subiecti**
Peter A	**Peter B**	iv, 7a. Be subject therefore to God
13. Be subject to every human ordinance for the Lord's sake **Code of Subordination** (to kings, governors, masters of slaves, husbands) iii, 8. All of one mind... humble-minded	v, 5. Be subject to the elders, and all to one another Prov. iii, 34 6. Humble yourselves... God...will exalt you	7b. (See below) 6. [Prov. iii, 34] 10. [Humble yourselves before the Lord...he will exalt you]
Vigilate		**Vigilate** (nil)
iv, 7. Be sober, therefore, and watch unto prayer... 11. If any one speaks, let it be as the words (*logia*) of God	8. Be sober, watch	
Resistite. State		**Resistite**
v, 8. Your adversary, the devil, goeth about as a roaring lion, seeking whom he may devour, 9. Whom resist, stedfast in the faith... 12. True grace, in which stand		7b. Resist the devil, and he will flee from you

like St Peter (*Deponentes*), to milk for babes, a comparison which is also known to St Paul (I Cor. iii, 2). His more advanced teaching occupies his first ten and a half chapters; but when he comes to the ethical part of his epistle, he falls back on the orthodox (Jewish) piety:

x, 19–25. Faith, hope, love.
    32–39. The need of endurance.
xi. Examples of faith considered as hope-endurance.
xii, 1. *Deponentes*, introducing the exhortation to endurance.
    9. *Subiecti*, to submit to the chastisement of God.
xiii, 1. Jewish ethical maxims, etc.
    18. *Vigilate*. The rulers of the church are represented as watching, as in Colossians; the hearers are asked to pray.

Taken individually the parallels with the texts we have studied may be slight, but it is at least an interesting fact that when the exposition of the need of endurance and the catalogue of its exemplars is finished, the exhortation to piety opens with the formula *Deponentes igitur omne*, and closes with a reference to watching and prayer.

Conclusion

These formulae seem, at first sight, to be commonplace phrases; they would not naturally be picked out as the leading thoughts of any of the documents in which they appear. Their appearance cannot be attributed to the literary influence of a dominant writer. They have only been found by careful comparison; and, when found, they hardly seem significant enough to repay investigation. Yet they did rise up in the mind of each writer in the same sequence, and at the same stage of thought. They follow one another in a predetermined order. There must be a reason for this; and the next step is to examine the words, and find out if they are as commonplace as they appear.

CHAPTER V
THE VOCABULARY OF THE PATTERN

SUMMARY OF CHAPTER V

The next step is to investigate the distribution of the Greek words which make up the pattern:

διὸ ἀποθέμενοι πᾶσαν κακίαν.
ὑποτάσσεσθε (ταπεινώθητε).
γρηγορεῖτε, ἀγρυπνεῖτε, νήψατε.
προσεύχεσθε.
στῆτε.
ἀντίστητε τῷ διαβόλῳ.

The first and last phrases are not found in the New Testament except in the passages we are studying; that is to say they belong to the pattern, and not otherwise to the individual writers, who use them here and here only. It is something more than a coincidence to find these phrases used once only by each author, and at the same point in the same thought sequence, especially as they never occur anywhere else in the New Testament.

On the whole the vocabulary is more suggestive of a common catechetical tradition than of any of the authors.

Other words which may belong to the tradition are

λόγος.
ἐπιθυμία.
στέφανος.
προσωπολημψία.
τέλειος.

CHAPTER V

THE VOCABULARY OF THE PATTERN

1. We have isolated four words or phrases which tend to occur in four documents (or five, if we divide Peter) in the same order. Not only so, but an examination of the context in which they occur justifies us in saying that they occur at the same logical point in each document, and with something of the same effect. The same series is also found in Hebrews, which raises the number of documents to six. Further parallelisms of thought and expression in our four primary documents also occur in close connection with the chosen phrases; but there is too much variation in order or expression to warrant us in including them at the present moment in our examination.

2. The next step is an investigation into the actual Greek words employed. They are set out in Table VI, which also includes the parallels from Hebrews, I Thessalonians, I Corinthians, and Romans in which we have seen reason to suspect the existence of baptismal *tōrāh*.

Deponentes

3. The verb *apotithesthai*[1] (put by, or put off) is used by five of our documents at this point, and is only found elsewhere in the New Testament in the similar passage Rom. xiii, 12, and in Acts vii, 58, where it is used in the sense of depositing or storing, and, curiously enough, of clothes; for in the six cases, where its use is figurative, it obviously has its second meaning of taking off clothes. In Lev. xvi, 23 (LXX) this verb is used of the high priest putting away the defiled robes when he has finished with the ceremonies of the atonement; so it is possible that the full meaning of the word here is taking off, putting away, and abandoning. In the New

---

1 ἀποτίθεσθαι. All New Testament occurrences listed in the table. In Matt. xiv, 3 (of shutting up John in prison) the text is uncertain.

TABLE VI. The vocabulary of the pattern.

	I Thess. I Cor.	Rom.	Col.	Eph.	Pet. A	Pet. B	Jas.	Heb.	
ἐπιθυμία	iv, 5	xiii, 14	iii, 5	iv, 22	ii, 11*		(iv, 1)*		* + στρατεύεσθαι (cf. Rom. vii, 23). Jas. has ἡδοναί
κτίζειν, etc.			iii, 10	iv, 24	(i, 23)		(i, 18)		Pet. has ἀπογεννᾶν: Jas. ἀποκύειν + κτίσμα.
ΑΠΟΤΙΘΕΣΘΑΙ		xiii, 12*	iii, 8	iv, 25	ii, 1		i, 21	xii, 1	*D.E. read ἀποβάλλειν. Eph. has a doublet (iv, 22, 25). Elsewhere in N.T. only Acts vii, 58, rejecting it in Matt. xiv, 3
κακία			iii, 8	iv, 31	ii, 1		i, 21		
(a) λόγος			i, 5	i, 13	ii, 2		i, 21	v, 11	λόγος, at this point, not in the Pauline epistles, but see Col. iii, 16: also Col. i, 5, Eph. i, 13
γάλα	iii, 2				ii, 2			v, 12	
(b) ἐνδύειν	v, 8	xiii, 12	iii, 10	iv, 24					The figurative use of ἐνδύειν is purely Pauline except Luke xxiv, 49
ὅπλα	(v, 8)	xiii, 12		vi, 11					
Worship		xii, 1	iii, 16	v, 20	ii, 5		i, 27		Remarkable variety of vocabulary. Cf. Mal. i, 11
ΥΠΟΤΑΣΣΕΙΝ (Social Code)	xvi, 16	xiii, 1	iii, 18	v, 21	v, 5		iv, 7	xii, 9	A 'Code of Subordination' is also found in the Two Ways, I Clem., Titus ii, 5ff., etc.
ταπεινοῦν			iii, 12	iv, 2	v, 6		iv, 10		
ΓΡΗΓΟΡΕΙΝ, etc.	v, 6f. xvi, 13	xiii, 11	iv, 2	(vi, 18)	(iv, 7)	v, 8	v, 8	(xiii, 17)	Eph. and Heb. ἀγρυπνεῖν. Pet. A, νηφεῖν. Pet. B νηφ. + γρηγ. These words only occur in epistles at points listed on table, except I Pet. i, 13, II Tim. iv, 5
προσεύχεσθαι			iv, 2	vi, 18	iv, 7			xiii, 18	
ΑΝΤΙΣΤΗΝΑΙ				vi, 13	v, 9		iv, 7		Only other figurative use, Matt. v, 39, 'Not to resist evil'
στῆναι	(xvi, 13)		iv, 12	vi, 11 f.	v, 12				This figurative use is Pauline, except I Pet. v, 12
διάβολος				vi, 11	v, 8		iv, 7		Eph. has a doublet (iv, 27, vi, 11). Never occurs elsewhere in the Epistles, except in Pastorals with a different meaning

Note. It will be noted that (a) and (b) represent alternative modes of continuing after ἀποτίθεσθαι: (b) is specifically Pauline (see Table III, p. 20), (a) would appear to be the original continuation: see note *ad hoc.*

Round brackets imply the use of a different Greek word: see note *ad hoc.*

Testament it is only used in these passages; it occurs once in each document, and at the same point in each. I find it also in I Clem. lvii, 1 and II Clem. i, 6, in a similar ethical sense. In Mart. Pol. xiii, 2 it is used of unclothing the martyr, which is, of course, a final unclothing.

4. In Romans, Colossians, and Ephesians, it is followed by the antithetical verb *enduein*, 'put on'. It is hard to see how, if the other writers were copying Paul, they could fail to reproduce the antithesis; but the word *enduein* does not occur in a figurative sense anywhere in the New Testament except in Paul, and in Luke xxiv, 49 of the reception of the Holy Spirit.

5. The word *kakia*[1] (badness, wickedness) is not very common: Matt. vi, 34 (a Jewish proverb?); Acts viii, 22; Rom. i, 29 and Tit. iii, 3, which are sin catalogues of the catechetical type; I Cor. v, 8 which is a passover formula; I Cor. xiv, 20 which alludes clearly to the *Deponentes* itself in its Petrine form ('it is with regard to *kakia* that ye are to be as little children'); and our four documents (twice in Peter, ii, 1 and ii, 16). It seems to be a word characteristic of Jewish traditional material rather than of the New Testament authors. Hermas, too, connects it with the child status; his second commandment says, 'Thou shalt be *akakos* like little children'; is not this still a third form of Peter's *Deponentes*, which couples 'putting off *kakia*' with being 'as new-born babes'? The whole phrase is, therefore, a distinctive one; it comes at the same point in each document, and nowhere else in the New Testament.

Subiecti

6. The word *hupotassein*[2] (to place in subjection or subordination) has a wide use outside the passages under study, and is characteristic of a Hebrew doctrine of submission to

1 κακία. All New Testament occurrences not given in the table are given above.

2 ὑποτάσσειν. In Luke of the child Jesus and his parents (in accordance with catechetical teaching) and in x, 17 and x, 20 of the demons. Elsewhere only in the epistles: (a) cosmic, based on Ps. viii, 6, cx, 1, I Cor. xv, 27ff., Eph. i, 22, Phil. iii, 21, Heb. ii, 5ff., I Pet. iii, 22; (b) of sacred

divine authority. It is not found outside the epistles except for three occurrences in Luke, one of which alludes to the duties of children. We may put on one side, first of all, a use of the word which is typical of dogmatic controversy in Paul and Hebrews and has to do with a sacred cosmic order; it is based on Ps. viii, 6 and cx, 1; it occurs once in Peter (iii, 22); it belongs to a specific theological argument, and is in the nature of a quotation from the Old Testament. As I Clement shows, however, this use of the word forms the real background for its use in our six occurrences and parallels in Titus and I Cor. xvi, 16; the sacred social order is part of the cosmic. Apart from these passages, it is used only in Paul: of subordination to the law (Rom. viii, 7), to vanity, i.e. idols (viii, 20), and to righteousness (x, 3); in I Cor. xiv, 32 and 34 it has to do with church order.

7. The word is not, then, by any means, peculiar to the parallel passages under examination. On the other hand, it is a distinctive feature of a type of exhortation which demands the subordination of the individual to the sacred social order and its leaders under God. In Romans, Colossians, Ephesians, Peter, and Titus, these passages have every appearance of being derived from Jewish *tōrāh*. Similar passages also marked by the use of this word are found in the *Two Ways* (Did. iv, 1) and in I Clem. i, 3 f. and 21, and in other post-apostolic writings. Clement alludes to this type of catechism as the 'code of subordination'. The word is clearly characteristic of a well-known type of catechetical material, and each writer felt that a reference to it at this point was appropriate.

8. The verb *tapeinoun*[1] (to humiliate or humble) is associated

authority in the social order: Rom. xiii, 1 ff., Eph. v, 21 ff., Col. iii, 18 ff., Tit. ii, 5 ff., I Pet. ii, 13 ff., v, 5; (c) of God: Heb. xii, 9, Jas. iv, 7; (d) miscellaneous: Rom. viii, 7 of the law, viii, 20 of vanity, i.e. idols, x, 3 of righteousness, I Cor. xiv, 32, 34, and xvi, 16 in connection with church order. This lists all New Testament occurrences.

1 ταπεινοῦν: (a) the humiliation-exaltation paradox: Matt. xviii, 4, xxiii, 12 (twice), Luke xiv, 11 (twice), xviii, 14 (twice); (b) quoting Isa. xl, 4: Luke iii, 5; (c) in Paul: II Cor. xi, 7, xii, 21, Phil. ii, 8, iv, 12, two of which are based on (a); (d) Jas. iv, 10 and I Pet. v, 6. This lists all New Testament occurrences.

with *hupotassein* not only in Peter B and James but with great frequency in I Clement. In the New Testament it is used fourteen times, almost always in connection with *hupsoun*, to exalt; here and in the other nine cases it probably quotes or refers to a well-known aphorism of Jewish *tōrāh* (cf. Ecclus. i, 30).

Vigilate

9. The word *grēgorein*[1] (keep awake) is used in its literal sense in the Marcan Gethsemane story (xiv. 34, 37, 38) and by Luke in an apocalyptic parable (xii, 37). In its figurative sense it is used in the Marcan apocalypse (xiii, 34, 35, 37), where the synonymous verb *agrupnein* also occurs (xiii, 33). In copying Mark, Matthew preserves the six cases of *grēgorein*, Luke preserves the one case of *agrupnein*. This accounts for all gospel cases of *grēgorein* (*agrupnein* is used elsewhere in a literal sense). In view of its apocalyptic colour we are not surprised to find *grēgorein* in Rev. iii, 2, iii, 3, and xvi, 15; but it is not used elsewhere in the New Testament except in the passages in the table, and in Acts xx, 31 where it occurs at the conclusion of a Pauline exhortation; curiously enough it is followed immediately by a reference to the 'word', as in Colossians, Ephesians, and Peter. Apart, then, from apocalypse (Mark and Revelation), the figurative use of *grēgorein* and *agrupnein* (regarding them as interchangeable) is confined to the passages in our table and to the similar Pauline passage in Acts xx, 31.

10. The word *nēphein* (be sober) is associated with (or substituted for) *grēgorein* in I Thess. v, 6, 8 and I Pet. i, 13, iv, 7, v, 8. This interesting fact is a minor point substantiating the connection between the two documents. Its only other use in the New Testament is II Tim. v, 5.

11. The command to keep awake or be sober is associated with prayer only in Mark xiv, 38, Colossians, Ephesians,

---

1 γρηγορεῖν, ἀγρυπνεῖν, νηφεῖν. All New Testament occurrences are given above except for ἀγρυπνεῖν in its literal sense.

Peter A, and Hebrews. Compare *agōnizesthai en tais pros-euchais*, Rom. xv, 30 and Col. iv, 12.

Resistite

12. The simple word *stēnai*[1] (to stand) is used in Colossians, Ephesians and Peter B, and the compound word *antistēnai* (to withstand or resist) in Ephesians, Peter B and James. (It will be observed that Ephesians and Peter B have both.)

13. Here, it may be said, is a colourless word 'stand' on which nothing at all can be built. If, however, we study the uses of the aorist intransitive form *stēnai* in the epistles, we find the results are interesting. In Hebrews and James it is only used of literal standing; but its ten uses in Paul and its one use in Peter are all of standing firm in the teaching or in the Christian status (faith, gospel, grace, etc.), except I Cor. vii, 37, where it has the allied meaning of a definite decision to adopt a permanent course of action in connection with the moral life; in I Cor. x, 12 it implies resistance to temptation. The allied word *stēkein*[2] occurs outside Paul in the literal sense, and seven times in Paul in the same figurative sense as *stēnai*; it seems to be a technical term for perseverance in the spiritual life.

14. An examination of the word *antistēnai*[3] gives interesting results. In its figurative sense of resisting evil, it is never used by any of our three authors except at this point; in fact it is only once used in this sense in the whole New Testament

1 στῆναι, aorist intransitive, in figurative sense referred to above: Rom. v, 2, xi, 20, I Cor. vii, 37, x, 12, xv, 1, II Cor. i, 24, Eph. vi, 11 ff., Col. iv, 12, I Pet. v, 12; other uses: II Tim. ii, 19 of a foundation, Heb. x, 11 of a priest, Jas. ii, 3 and v, 9 in the literal sense. This lists all occurrences in the epistles.

2 στήκειν: Mark xi, 25 plus προσευχόμενοι. Otherwise only in Rom. xiv, 4, I Cor. xvi, 13, Gal. v, 1, Phil. i, 27, iv, 1, I Thess. iii, 8, II Thess. ii, 15, all figurative as above.

3 ἀντιστῆναι: (a) in literal sense: Luke xxi, 15, Acts vi, 10, xiii, 8, Gal. ii, 11, Rom. ix, 19, xiii, 2 (of God), II Tim. iii, 8 (of Moses), iii, 8 (the truth), iv, 15 (our words); (b) figuratively: Matt. v, 39 (of evil), Eph. vi, 13, Jas. iv, 7, I Pet. v, 9 (all of the devil). This lists all New Testament occurrences.

THE VOCABULARY OF THE PATTERN

apart from these passages, and there the hearer is told *not* to resist evil (Matt. v, 39)! It is a hapax-legomenon for James and Peter.

15. The word *diabolos*[1] is a hapax-legomenon for each of the three authors. St Paul uses the term Satan or tempter elsewhere; but in Peter and James there is no mention of the evil one except in this passage. In Ephesians its use in vi, 11 is anticipated in iv, 27; but St Paul never uses it elsewhere. Indeed St James' theory of temptation (i, 13 ff.) might seem to exclude the conception of a tempter. The form of the saying in James agrees with that in *Testaments* (Test. Nap. viii, 4, cf. Mand. xii, v, 2).

16. Now the mere appearance of the word *diabolos* once in each author would not be a fact of much significance; but some degree of significance must be attributed to its appearance at the same logical point. This coincidence becomes much more striking when we note its conjunction with the word *antistēnai*, to resist; for the counsel to 'resist the devil' is not found elsewhere in the New Testament. Its appearance here in each writer can hardly be accidental. But when we consider that this coincidence is only one in a series of coincidences, of which we have examined four, and that they occur so nearly in the same order in each document, the possibility of chance vanishes. The chances against four points appearing in a given order are 24 to 1. There must be a reason for this series appearing as it does.

17. Further, the four points are merely the four most striking points in a series of similarities which cannot always be established by the unanimous witness of all the documents; and if we add merely one more point (e.g. 'new birth' or 'new creation') the figure 24 becomes 120. Such mathematical calculations have no scientific value, applied as they are to phenomena which are not wholly within the realm of

1 διάβολος: not in Mark, six times in Matthew, six in Luke, three in John, two in Acts, four in I John, one in Jude, five in Revelation; in the Pastorals it probably means 'slanderer'. Otherwise only in Eph. iv, 27, vi, 11, Heb. ii, 14, Jas. iv, 7, I Pet. v, 8.

pure chance; but they serve to illustrate the enormous probability (amounting to certainty) that the common pattern is prior to, and independent of, any of our authors.

Summary

18. The four phrases we have been considering have an interesting distribution in the New Testament.

Deponentes. The phrase 'putting off all evil' is only found at this point in our four main authorities. The verb *apotithesthai* is only found at this point in the table of parallels except for Acts vii, 58. The noun *kakia* is not common in the New Testament, and is used in passages which seem to derive from catechetical formulae, or other Jewish traditional material.

Subiecti. The word *hupotassein* is used in passages which deal with a sacred order, cosmic or social. In three of our documents it introduces what can only be regarded as Jewish catechetical material. In the other two it is combined with Prov. iii, 34 and the humiliation-exaltation paradox (cf. Ecclus. i, 30); the combination also suggests Jewish catechism.

Vigilate. The words *grēgorein* and *agrupnein* are used in the gospels and in apocalyptic; the only uses in the epistles are at this point in the pattern, and the parallels shown in the table. *Nēphein* is practically peculiar to this point on our table; it only occurs once in the New Testament elsewhere. *Antistēnai* is found elsewhere in Paul; but *diabolos* is found nowhere else in these authors.

Resistite. *Stēnai* is common in Paul in the sense of standing firm in the faith and the new status it confers, and is used in this sense at this point in Colossians, Ephesians, and Peter B. In the rest of the New Testament it is used only in a literal sense. The command to 'resist the devil' is only found here in the whole New Testament; but it is also found in *Testaments* and Hermas, and would therefore seem to be a familiar phrase in the catechetical literature of Greek Judaism.

19. It must be admitted that the vocabulary is more distinctive than might have been anticipated. While *stēnai* and *hupotassein* are common elsewhere, especially in Paul, they are used in a peculiar way in passages which seem to derive from or refer to the catechesis; *kakia* definitely belongs to this type of literature; *grēgorein* and *agrupnein* are peculiar to these parallel passages so far as the epistles are concerned, and 'put off all evil' and 'resist the devil' are not found elsewhere in the New Testament.

Associated Words

20. There are other words which seem to associate themselves with this pattern as we study it; but they fail to appear in the same position in each of our authorities.

(*a*) *Logos.* A reference to the 'word' accompanied by the concepts of 'truth' and 'salvation' is associated with the *Deponentes* in James and Peter A, but occurs much earlier in Colossians and Ephesians. Except in Ephesians it is also associated with the ideas of growth or of a seed.

(*b*) *Epithumia.*[1] This word, usually translated 'lust', represents the Hebrew *yetser*, or evil inclination; it tends to occur at the opening of the paraenesis, or of a section of it. It is often in close association with some word representing the Hebrew word *halākāh*, 'walking'; and the reference is usually to gentile behaviour, or behaviour prior to conversion. In Peter A and James such an instance follows the *Deponentes* (Pet. ii, 11 = Jas. iv, 1 and iii, 13); in Ephesians it precedes (iv, 3 and 22); in Colossians it also precedes, and is conflated with, the three sins of uncleanness (iii, 5–7), as it is in I Thess. iv, 5. The collocation of 'walking' and *epithumiai* is also found

---

1 ἐπιθυμία: not characteristic of the gospels: Mark iv, 19, Luke xxii, 15, John viii, 44, only. In the epistles, Rom. i, 24, vi, 12, vii 8 (twice), xiii, 14, Gal. v, 16, v, 24, Eph. ii, 3, iv, 22, Phil. i, 23, Col. iii, v, I Thess. ii, 17 (in a good sense as in Luke), iv, 5, Jas. i, 14, i, 15, I Pet. i, 14, ii, 10, iv, 2, iv, 3: almost all in the sense expounded above. Also four times in II Peter, three in I John, two in Jude, one in Revelation. This lists all New Testament occurrences.

in Gal. v, 16, Eph. ii, 3, Pet. iv, 2, 3. In Peter A and James the word for 'walking' is *anastrophe*;[1] in Paul usually the verbal form *peripatein*.[2]

(c) *Stephanos*.[3] The promise of the crown is found early in the pattern in James (i, 12) and Peter B (v, 4). It is clearly alluded to in II Tim. iv, 8, and quoted in Rev. ii, 10. It was a well-known saying in the Christian tradition.

(d) *Prosōpolēmpsia*.[4] This strange word is a combination of *prosōpon* and *lambanein* and means 'receiving the person', or 'favouritism'. Some form of this word (which is a Hebraism) occurs once in each of our documents; otherwise only twice in the New Testament, Rom. ii, 11, and Acts x, 34, which, curiously enough, is the account of the first gentile baptism. In Peter A and James, the word is associated with the law of brotherly love (Lev. xix, 18); in Colossians, Ephesians, and the *Two Ways* (Did. iv, 10) it is part of the code of social subordination which follows the *Subiecti*. Its occurrence here may, perhaps, be connected with Lev. xix, 15; but it is a commonplace in Hebrew.

(e) *Teleios*.[5] This word is absent in Peter, but is found in other New Testament writers, and is a favourite of St Paul

---

1 ἀναστροφή: Gal. i, 13, Eph. iv, 22, I Tim. iv, 12, Heb. xiii, 7, Jas. iii, 13, I Pet. i, 15, i, 18, ii, 12, iii, 1, iii, 2, iii, 16, II Pet. ii, 7, iii, 11. ἀναστρέφειν: four times in gospels and Acts in literal sense; figuratively in II Cor. i, 12, Eph. ii, 3, I Tim. iii, 15, Heb. x, 33, xiii, 18, I Pet. i, 17, II Pet. ii, 18. This lists all New Testament occurrences.

2 περιπατεῖν (omitting synoptic gospels and Acts): thirty-three times in Paul always in the figurative sense, once in Hebrews (xiii, 9), once in I Peter (v, 8) of the devil (!), thirty-two times in the Johannine books.

3 στέφανος: in this sense, I Cor. ix, 25, II Tim. iv, 8, Jas. i, 12, I Pet. v, 4, and eight times in Revelation. στεφανοῦν: II Tim. ii, 5, Heb. ii, 7, ii, 9 (from Ps. viii, 6).

4 προσωπολήμπτης, Acts x, 34; ἀπροσωπολήμπτως, I Pet. i, 17; προσωπολημψία, Rom. ii, 11, Eph. vi, 9, Col. iii, 25, Jas. ii, 1; προσωπολημπτεῖν, Jas. ii, 9; πρόσωπον λαμβάνειν, Mark xii, 14, Gal. ii, 6; cf. θαυμάζοντες πρόσωπα, Jude 16.

5 τέλειος: three times in Matthew, v, 48 (twice), xix, 21. Elsewhere only in Rom. xii, 2, I Cor. ii, 6, xiii, 10, xiv, 20, Eph. iv, 13, Phil. iii, 15, Col. i, 28, iv, 12, Heb. v, 14, ix, 11 (of the tabernacle), Jas. i, 4 (twice), i, 17, i, 25, iii, 2, I John iv, 18; the Chester-Beatty papyrus is peculiar in giving it in I Cor. i, 8. τελειότης: Col. iii, 14, Heb. vi, 1.

who uses it of the adult man, the mature product of wisdom; it is the culmination of the process of education in the fear of the Lord, and therefore the antithesis of the child status of the neophyte. The Hebrew word *tām*, which it may sometimes represent, as for instance in Matt. v, 48, seems to denote integrity whether moral or physical; this sense of the word, therefore, connects rather with the Levitical conception 'without spot or blemish'.

These words and phrases are presented here as examples of the kind of vocabulary which was in use in the Christian didactic tradition, and is characteristic of it in the documents we are studying.

21. The reader will note that where there is divergence in vocabulary or order, Colossians and Ephesians are usually found on one side, and Peter and James on the other. On the other hand, there are contacts between Peter and the Pauline epistles which are not found in James; these contacts are with Ephesians (I Thessalonians and Romans), not, on the whole, with Colossians. There are characteristic features of Ephesians (I Thessalonians and Romans) which are not represented in Colossians, James or Peter; we may particularly note the lyrical passages based on light and darkness and the spiritual armour, which have parallels in *Testaments* and Hermas, and seem ultimately based on the second Isaiah. The common pattern is not therefore to be explained as a reproduction of Paul.

SUMMARY OF CHAPTER VI

The next step is to abstract these formulae from the documents in which they occur, and study them as a connected thought sequence apart from the individual documents.

1. *Introductory.*

(*a*) The prayer for wisdom and knowledge.

(*b*) The warning about temptation, and the virtue of endurance.

(*c*) The avoidance of gentile sins: the three major sins: the evil inclination.

(*d*) The word of truth which can save the soul.

(*e*) The new birth (or creation) by the word.

2. *The Paraenesis.*

(*a*) *Deponentes.* The command to put off evil and guile (Ps. xxxiv, 13) introduces varying commands as to catechumen behaviour, all culminating in a pure and spiritual worship (a neo-levitical phrase) offered to God and the Father.

(*b*) *Subiecti.* The catechumen is not only to be submissive to God but also to the elders; an extension of the honour due to fathers which in Jewish catechisms follows the command to honour God.

(*c*) *Vigilate.* The command to submit is associated with a command to humble oneself, which in Jewish thought suggests fasting, which in turn leads naturally to the thought of prayer. But the word 'watch' (gospels and apocalypse) has a suggestion of temptations and afflictions to come.

(*d*) *Resistite.* We thus come to the combat with evil: but *State* also suggests standing upright and perfect as in Jewish *tōrāh*. Are they alternative endings?

CHAPTER VI

THE COMMON PATTERN

1. If the pattern which runs through our main authorities is of independent origin, it should be possible to show a thought sequence running through it which is characteristic of itself, and does not derive from any of the writers who reproduce it.

Introductory

2. The prayer for wisdom and knowledge, common to Paul and James,[1] would naturally precede sessions of instruction.

3. In Ecclesiasticus and the Jewish rite of proselyte baptism, the comer is warned of temptation or adversity;[2] but I think we may assert that it is only in the Christian documents that he is told to rejoice,[3] exult, or boast in his trials and afflictions. The emphasis on hope-endurance is as old as Ecclus. ii; but the addition of love in some Christian documents would appear to anticipate or recall other instruction. The conception of testing of faith (as in a furnace) is also found in Ecclus. ii. The crown is found as early as Proverbs (i, 9).[4]

---

1 Eph. i, 17, Col. i, 9, Jas. i, 5.

2 'Why dost thou come to be made a proselyte? Knowest thou not that Israel is afflicted, buffeted, humiliated, and harried, and that sufferings and sore trials come upon them?' Quoted by F. L. Gavin, *Jewish Antecedents*.

3 E.g. I Thess. i, 6. Adumbrated in Ecclus. ii, 4.

4 The crown in Prov. i, 9, iv, 9, etc., is wisdom itself; with this use is naturally connected the idea of the crown of white hairs of the elder. There is also the turban of the high priest, whose regalia is already interpreted spiritually in Testaments (Test. Levi, viii) in a way which closely resembles the spiritual armour of Eph. vi. R. Simeon in Aboth iv, 17 says there are three crowns: of *tōrāh*, of priesthood, of the kingdom. The crown is, however, a common symbol in the ancient world (e.g. in athletics, I Cor. ix, 25, II Tim. iv, 8), and Krauss says that crowns were awarded in the synagogue to persons of outstanding piety: *Synagogale Altertümer*.

4. A reference of a neo-levitical type to a renunciation of the sins of uncleanness (sometimes three deadly sins, sometimes merely 'vanity' or gentile customs) would seem to be found where gentile converts are to be dealt with. It is strongly emphasised in Paul, alluded to in Peter, and entirely missing in James which is Jewish-Christian.

5. All our documents, however, refer to the inward *epithumia* or evil inclination (the *yetser* of Rabbinic moral theology); and there seems to have existed in the teaching tradition a formula which asserts that it (or they) carries on war against the soul. The reference may be combined with the neo-levitical formula of the sins against holiness, or it may stand alone. It is often connected with the Jewish phrase 'how to walk', or 'your conversation' (*halākāh*).

6. The word (or the truth) or, in Paul, the gospel is an important feature of the pattern. The testimony of Acts and I Thessalonians shows that in the first period of the Christian mission the initial act of faith was referred to as 'receiving the word'. *Logos* seems earlier than *euangelion* for the Christian message; and so is the verb 'evangelise'[1] (Isa. LXX), which is characteristic of Peter, whereas *euangelion* is not.[2] In Colossians and Ephesians the reference to the word comes early in the epistle; in Peter and James it is part of the *Deponentes*; in three cases it is associated with the word 'save' or 'salvation'; in three with seed or growing.

7. The new birth or new creation is associated with the *Deponentes* in all four documents. It is a well-known fact that St Paul avoids using the vocabulary of the new birth,

1 We may follow Peter in connecting this usage of words with Isa. xl, 6 (quoted both in Peter and James); the same chapter uses the word εὐαγγελίζεσθαι. For 'receiving the word', see for instance Acts ii, 41, viii, 14, xi, 1 and I Thess. i, 6. A study of I Thessalonians suggests that λόγος means the Christian message and its content in general, while εὐαγγέλιον (at this early stage) connotes the message in its presentation to the gentiles.

2 I Pet. iv, 17. The single occurrence here, like the single occurrence (for all Johannine writings) in Rev. xiv, 6, seems to suggest the announcement of God's judgment on the world, not the proclamation of Jesus as often in Paul.

preferring either dying and rising with Christ or a new creating; but his reference to converts as babes to be fed on milk[1] shows that in the Thessalonian period the new-birth language was well known in his churches; and he compares himself to a father who has begotten children, or even to a mother who brings them to birth.[2] St James, on the other hand, associates the noun *ktisma* (creation) with the birth by a word.

8. The creation background of baptism must be dealt with in another chapter; we merely note that there is a form of the Jewish rite of proselyte baptism which refers at this point to the creation of the world by a word.[3] In Christian documents two conceptions of the creative or procreative word are involved:

(*a*) The word as the agent in creation (Light).

(*b*) The word inducing birth, growth, fruit (Seed).

The Four-point Pattern

9. *Deponentes Igitur*. The striking word *apotithesthai* suggests stripping off clothes before baptism.[4] It is only St Paul who sees in them the symbol of the old self (old man) which is abandoned, and goes on to the thought of clothing oneself[5] with the new self, or with Christ, or with the whole armour of God.

10. St Peter says that the new converts desire, as new-born

1 I Cor. iii, 1.

2 Gal. iv, 19, I Cor. iv, 14–16. It would appear that St Paul is here comparing himself with Moses (Num. xi, 12) as he did earlier to Bezaleel. The Corinthian letters continually refer to Exodus-Numbers or to a midrash thereon.

3 'I am not worthy of him who spake the word, and the world came into existence': *Gerim*. Yebamoth merely has 'I am not worthy'. Cf. F. L. Gavin, *op. cit.*

4 The word ἐνδύειν, which follows this clause in Paul, makes it clear that the reference is to clothes; the middle voice implies something put off oneself.

5 ἐνδύειν: in the figurative sense: only in Luke xxiv, 49 and Paul, Rom. xiii, 12, xiii, 14, I Cor. xv, 53 (twice), xv, 54, II Cor. v, 3, Gal. iii, 27, Eph. iv, 24, vi, 11, vi, 14, Col. iii, 10, iii, 12, I Thess. v, 8. The symbolic uses in Revelation are related to the Pauline use, but go back to liturgical passages in the Old Testament, such as Psalms, Wisdom, 2 Isaiah. See p. 86, n. 1.

babes, the 'guileless'[1] milk of the word, and James urges them
to receive the word with meekness. These formulae suggest
the childlike qualities required of the learner, and St James
actually goes on to virtues necessary in a 'hearer'.

11. In Ephesians the convert is to put away the *pseudos* and
to speak truth; in Colossians simply *mē pseudesthai*. *Pseudos*[2]
is translated 'lying' in the A.V. but probably corresponds to
the 'guile' of Peter, and the 'hypocrisy' of Ecclus. i, 29;
Colossians then goes on to inculcate mercy, kindness, humble-
ness, meekness, long-suffering, though in Ephesians these
catechumen virtues have been introduced at an earlier point
(see Table V, pp. 42–3). The impression is that the sequence of
Colossians is more likely to be original. The vices and virtues
of the original pattern are probably those of speech; Ephesians
has 'put off lying, speak truth'; Colossians adds 'out of your
mouth'; James has 'slow to speak, slow to anger'.

12. 'To depart from evil' is a natural initial thought in any
treatment of the 'fear of the Lord'; but it may be conjectured
that the original base of this teaching is the catechumen
psalm (xxxiv)[3] quoted in Peter, and alluded to in Rom. xii:

11. Come ye children, hearken unto me:
     I will teach you fear of the Lord...
13. Let him refrain his tongue from evil:
     And his lips that they speak no guile.
14. Let him eschew evil, and do good:
     Let him seek peace, and ensue it.
                    (Quoted in I Pet. iii, 10f.)

13. The references to forbearance, forgiveness, love, and
peace in Colossians and Ephesians look original; but in Peter
and James the doctrine of sacred love is treated in another
section.

1 ἄδολος (without guile) balances the δόλος (guile) which is 'put off'.
2 ψεῦδος like μάταιος represents an application to ethics of terminology
first applied to idolatry. These formulae are based on the primal renunciation of Hebrew religion, a turning from idols ('false', 'vain') to a
'living' and 'true' God. Cf. I Thess. i, 9, Acts xiv, 15, I John v, 20.
3 Klein attaches great importance to this psalm in his treatment of
Rom. xii and xiii and I Peter: *Der älteste Katechismus.*

14. On the other hand the references to worship in all four are striking because of their very diversity of vocabulary; the verbal unlikeness draws attention to the agreement in thought sequence. It is as if such a reference had a natural place here. The phrase 'God (and) the Father' is common to Ephesians, Colossians, and James; and an emphasis on the Fatherhood of God is appropriate.[1] The song, music, and thanksgiving of Ephesians and Colossians closely resemble the detail of the account of speaking with tongues in I Corinthians.[2] They sound like an original element in the pattern, and harmonise with it in being acts of speech. The 'pure worship' of James, and the 'spiritual sacrifices' of Peter A, are other forms of the 'reasonable service' of Rom. xii, 1, and are based no doubt on Mal. i, 11, a text often quoted in post-apostolic literature.

15. *Subiecti Estote.* The command to be subject, if it follows the reference to worship, would more easily apply to God (as in James and Hebrews) than to the elders; the pendant 'be humbled' in Peter B and James certainly applies to God.[3] But this section has been enlarged in Colossians, Ephesians, and Peter A by the insertion of a catechism, based on the idea of subordination to the elders, which all seem to derive from a common source. Peter A includes the king, as does Rom. xiii, 1 by implication;[4] Peter B only mentions the

1 Because the newly baptised are now sons: cf. I Pet. i, 17, 'If you invoke as Father him who etc.' Cf. Gal. iv, 6, Rom. viii, 15.

2 I Cor. xiv, 15: προσεύξομαι τῷ πνεύματι...ψαλῶ...εὐχαριστίᾳ; Eph. v, 18ff.: ἐν πνεύματι...ψαλμοῖς...εὐχαριστοῦντες; Eph. vi, 18: προσευχόμενοι τῷ πνεύματι; and parallels in Col. iii, 16f., iv, 2 and 3.

3 In this section St Peter and St James are clearly reproducing exactly the same *tōrāh*, which is of a Jewish character, quoting Prov. iii, 34, Test. Nap. viii, 4 (in James), and the humiliation-exaltation paradox.

4 It is seldom recognised that the king is not mentioned in Rom. xiii, 1 ff., which could be purely Palestinian, and apply to the authorities of the Jewish state. This *tōrāh* about the civil authority (ἐξουσία, cf. *rashut*) is Jewish in tone (cf. Aboth i, 10, etc.), and concludes in both epistles with the law of love (Lev. xix, 18). St Peter then adds the code of subordination to the elders (versions of which are found in Ephesians, Colossians, Titus, Clement, *Two Ways*, etc.), concluding with general counsels of mutual forbearance which closely resemble Rom. xii, I Thess. v.

elders; Ephesians, like Peter B, adds 'all of you be subject to one another'. The twin conceptions are those of the community indwelt by the divine presence, and of the godlike status of the elders and fathers.[1] To humble oneself before the holy community and its holy rulers is to humble oneself before God.[2] If the original (Jewish?) pattern was connected with the initiation of disciples into a holy tradition of *tōrāh*, we may suspect that the base of this section was a command to be subject to the elders as to the Lord.

16. *Vigilate.* A command to watch and pray might naturally follow a command to submit oneself (to God) and humble oneself; to humble oneself is a Jewish synonym for fasting. But the word 'watch' in the gospels and apocalypse has to do with approaching affliction and persecution, the prospect of suffering and martyrdom, or the coming of the Lord.

17. *State.* Standing, in Jewish custom, is the posture of prayer; it is also a word which means continuance, perseverance, uprightness, righteousness. Job was 'upright and perfect',[3] a phrase very close to the 'stand perfect' of Colossians. Perfection is the objective of Christian morals, not only in the Sermon on the Mount (Matthew) but in all our documents except Peter; it suggests maturity (as opposed to the child-status of the convert) rather than assimilation to an absolute standard.[4]

18. *Resistite.* Standing also suggests standing firm, or

1 Lev. xix, 32.

2 It is this type of teaching which is repeated by St Ignatius, and attributed to divine authority. E.g. 'The Spirit proclaimed, saying: Apart from the bishop do nothing: guard your flesh as the temple of God: love the unity (i.e. love the brotherhood): flee from divisions: become imitators of Jesus Christ, as he is of the Father': Trall. vii, 2. St Ignatius is probably quoting catechetical *tōrāh* recast in the idiom of his *ekklēsia*.

3 Job i, 1: 'Perfect, upright, fearing the Lord, departing from evil.' According to Klein (*op. cit.*) *sûr mērā*, to turn from evil, is a tabloid formula for the whole *tōrāh*. The *Deponentes*, 'putting off all evil', is a form of this formula.

4 The word τέλειος, 'perfect', does not have to be explained from the 'mystery religions'; as stated above, it is characteristically Jewish. See p. 56, n. 1. Like σοφία, it is a Jewish term common in Paul, but missing in Peter.

standing one's ground. Hence the picture of the mature Christian as a warrior victorious in the contest with the devil. Here also is a touch of apocalyptic. It would appear possible that we have here a formula drawn from old Jewish catechetical tradition, upon which the apocalyptic conception has been superimposed.

SUMMARY OF CHAPTER VII

The *tōrāh* or catechetical instruction is given in the holy community, synagogue or *ekklēsia*, which assembles under its elders, who are given divine honour as fathers.

By the first century A.D. the rabbinic schools have been developed, with teaching elders (*tannāīm*) in regular succession; these fathers shared the divine honour, and eventually became more important than the elders of the local community.

A similar tannaite system is found in Christianity; didactic systems in Papias, Irenaeus, and Matthew.

St John, disciple and elder: 'The Elder.'

St Paul as the *tannā* of the gentiles.

St Peter as an elder.

The post-apostolic succession.

CHAPTER VII

THE SOCIAL-RELIGIOUS UNIT

1. It has been premised that the synagogue (*'edah*) is in its origin and essence nothing but the whole congregation of Israel, gathered before God, the most solemn place for this assembly being the gate of the sanctuary; the Christian word *ekklēsia*[1] (church) is practically identical in meaning, representing as it does the word *kāhāl* in the LXX. It was to such an assembly that the *tōrāh* of Lev. xix was to be promulgated; and the basis of this *tōrāh* is the holy presence indwelling the community and sanctifying all its relationships.

The Elders

2. The community was assembled before God under its legitimate leaders, the elders (*zākēn*, pl. *z'kēnīm*), an institution which is traced back to the period of Mt Sinai,[2] and is as old and as sacred as the *tōrāh* itself. Since walking in the way of the Lord is rewarded by long life and many children, it is clear that the elders and fathers are the natural exemplars and exponents of this holy wisdom.

3. The godly man like Job, 'perfect and upright', is the ideal mature man, and therefore resembles God himself, as Blake rightly emphasised in his illustrations to Job. In Daniel[3] and Enoch, God is an elder with the crown of white hairs; in *Mekilta* he descends on Mt Sinai 'like an elder, full

1 The word ἐκκλησία is not used in Peter or James. James uses συναγωγή (ii, 2); Did. iv, 14 uses ἐκκλησία, but not Barn.; both words probably mean the holy assembly. Peter prefers ἀδελφότης, 'brotherhood', or οἶκος θεοῦ, 'house of God', which suggests both family and temple (ii, 5).

2 Exod. xviii, Num. xi.

3 Dan. vii, 9: an 'ancient of days', i.e. an old man. The white hair was the crown of the elder; the phrase sufficed by itself to indicate an elder: Lev. xix, 32, 'Before the white hairs thou shalt rise up, and honour the face of the aged, and fear thy God: I the Lord.'

⟨ 67 ⟩   5-2

of compassion'; it is a title closely allied to that of father. Fathers and elders, therefore, are to receive honour and fear of the same kind as is offered to God.[1] The oldest form of the so-called *haustafel*[2] must have been that fathers, husbands, and masters of slaves (identical persons of course) were to be honoured as the Lord,[3] which is the implication of the fifth commandment.

4. Now in the first century A.D. a distinction had arisen between elders who were capable of handling *tōrāh* and those who were not.[4] A similar distinction had arisen between the ancient institution of the synagogue and the newer institution of the rabbinic school, the beginnings of which are seen in Proverbs and Ecclesiasticus; but even here the authority of the teacher is his position in the succession of the fathers.[5] The teaching elders of Israel (*tannāīm*) achieved an overwhelming superiority in the nation, and worked out a holy pedigree of a didactic type back to the 'Great Synagogue' of Ezra, and behind that, through the prophets, to Moses and the seventy elders appointed at Sinai.[6] It is a succession of

1 See p. 4, n. 2.

2 For the *haustafel*, see W. L. Clarke, *New Testament Problems*, pp. 157ff., and J. C. Wand on I Peter in the Westminster series. The German word indicates a code of duties exhibiting the relations of the members of a family or tribe; such a conception is inadequate to describe the codes of Jewish *tōrāh* whose basis is the honour paid to fathers and elders as visible emblems of deity.

3 E.g. *Two Ways*, 'as to a pattern of God' (Did. iv, 11); Eph. v, 22, 'as to the Lord'; vi, 1, 'in the Lord' (if the text is secure); vi, 5, 'as to Christ'. The phrases as found in Ephesians are softened in Colossians and Peter, but the word 'fear' implies the same thought, I Pet. i, 17, ii, 18, iii, 2, iii, 14, iii, 15, Eph. v, 21, vi, 5, Did. iv, 8, iv, 10, iv, 11. The fear of the Lord includes the fear of the fathers of the community; mothers share the divine honour, I Pet. iii, 7, I Tim. iii, 11, v, 2, Tit. ii, 3.

4 I Tim. v, 17. This epistle seems to distinguish the bishop and deacon (who are of the tannaite class?) from the elders, who are primarily the fathers of the community, the προιστάμενοι of I Thess. v, 12, the ἡγούμενοι of Heb. xiii. Confusion arises because (a) the word elder in its honorific sense may be applied to any outstanding *tannā*, and (b) the plural ἐπίσκοποι may be applied, as in Philippians, I Clement and *Didache*, to include church authorities (not deacons) of either class.

I cannot think that B. S. Easton is right in extending the word 'elder' to include the deacons.

5 E.g. Prov. iv, 1–4.   6 See *Pirke Aboth* i.

the word or *tōrāh*, passed on from generation to generation with the laying on of hands; a specialised plural, *'ābōth*, was invented to denote spiritual fathers of the didactic succession. A unique position in this succession is occupied by R. Hillel, who is called in an absolute sense 'the elder'; and it is explained that the word *zākēn* really means *zēh s'kānāh ḥokmāh*, 'he who has acquired wisdom'.[1] From the fall of Jerusalem in A.D. 70 this tannaite succession ruled Israel; it became a patriarchate.

Tannaite Elders in Christianity

5. It would appear that a similar development took place within Christianity. We have the leaders of the congregation or elders of the original type;[2] we also find a superior ministry, apostolic, prophetic, and rabbinic, who may be thought of as elders in the tannaite sense.[3] According to Papias and Irenaeus a full tannaite system of elders and disciples existed in Asia Minor, deriving their succession from the disciple John (called, like Hillel, *the* Elder), and from other disciples of the Lord; they even visualise the Lord himself as an elder.[4] In the Matthaean school we have another didactic system, though the actual word 'teacher' or 'rabbi' or 'elder(?)' is forbidden,

1 Quoted by Hertz, *Pentateuch and Haftorahs* to Lev. xix, 32.

2 E.g. Rom. xii, 6ff. mentions seven functions of leadership and service within the community: prophecy, ministry, teaching, exhorting, apportioning shares (at the meal?), presiding, bestowing alms. 'Ministry' in Paul, διακονία, seems to be a general term denoting an official ministry of assistance usually in a subordinate capacity; it is probably used here as a term antithetical to prophecy, which by its nature cannot constitute an office. See also Tit. ii, 5ff. for community elders.

3 I Cor. xii, 28ff. deals with spiritual gifts, not with official ministries in the community, though of course the two may frequently co-exist in the same person, and the first be necessary to the second; in the first class (which we may compare with the tannaite order) come apostles, prophets, and teachers; in a lower grade come gifts of healing, functions of assistance, functions of government, and kinds of tongues. Eph. iv, 11 expands the higher order into apostles, prophets, evangelists, shepherds and teachers.

4 Rev. i, 14, 'The hairs of his head white as wool.' In Irenaeus, *Adv. Haer.* ii, 32, we are informed that the elders of the Johannine school argued (against Luke?) that Jesus must have been over forty; for how could he teach, not having reached the age of a teacher? With which harmonises John viii, 57.

on the authority of a tradition received from the Lord himself.[1] There is evidence, therefore, that one element of great importance in the Christian *ekklēsia* was the propagation of *tōrāh* by teachers who had received it in true succession, and that the process was oral.

6. St Paul is regarded in post-apostolic times as the great *tannā* of the gentiles; it is wisdom (*hokmāh*) for which he is renowned; 'he taught the whole world wisdom', says Clement.[2] This view finds ample confirmation in our first document, Colossians. It is progress in 'wisdom' and 'knowledge' which he specially desires for the new converts; and his own peculiar function is a ministry of the word to the gentiles, in which he 'admonishes' and 'teaches' every man in all 'wisdom' so as to establish every man 'perfect' in Christ.[3] In this and in other epistles he makes a definite claim to such jurisdiction over the gentile world, and in Philemon it is possible that he actually calls himself an elder (*presbutēs*).[4]

7. He also allows us to see a staff of fellow-workers or 'deacons' (*diakonoi*)[5] who work with and under him. Three are Jews; but Epaphras, a 'faithful deacon of Christ on our

1 Matt. xxiii, 8–10 forbids 'rabbi', 'father', and καθηγητής. Mark x, 43 (and consequently Matt. xx, 26) discourages μέγας (rab?) and πρῶτος in favour of διάκονος and δοῦλος; Luke xxii, 26 discourages μείζων (elder?) and ἡγούμενος as compared with νεώτερος and διακονῶν. It is possible that a similar disclaimer is to be found in passages like Ign. Eph. iii, Polyc. iii, Barn. i, 8, II Clem. xviii, 2.

2 I Clem. v, 7, II Pet. iii, 15.

3 Col. i, 25ff.

4 Philem. ix: πρεσβύτης. There is much to commend this interpretation. Its conjunction with διατάσσειν suggests that it carries a lot of authority. Its primary meaning is simply 'aged' as in Luke i, 18. In Tit. ii, 2 it is the equivalent of πρεσβύτερος in Timothy. It is applied to Polycarp in Mart. Pol. vii, 2, vii, 3; and to the teacher who initiated St Justin Martyr into the faith (*Dial.*), 'παλαιός τις πρεσβύτης', where παλαιός would be redundant if πρεσβύτης simply meant aged. Here, as in Philemon, it seems to mean the ideal aged man who is a repository of and teacher of wisdom.

5 διάκονος in Paul means one who has an official position of service and assistance, διακονία. The apostle is a διάκονος of Christ; his staff is composed of his own διάκονοι; and there are also διάκονοι who are associated with the local ἐπίσκοποι in Phil. i, 1.

behalf',[1] seems to be a Greek; it was under authoritative direction from St Paul that he evangelised the Lycus valley (with Archippus, St Paul's fellow-campaigner?) and it is St Paul who sends Tychicus in his place. All seems to be organised and authoritative; the epistle leaves as clear an impression on this point as it does on the importance of adhering to the teaching formulae which had been received by the converts.

8. St Peter undoubtedly calls himself an elder,[2] and indicates Mark as 'his son',[3] by which we may understand his successor in the didactic system. Silvanus is commended as 'a faithful brother',[4] a phrase which gives him perhaps a tannaite status as a colleague of St Peter. He appears to have a definite sphere of jurisdiction, like the apostolic subordinates in Colossians; and this region is by no means the same as that of St Paul.[5] St Peter does not use the words 'wisdom' and 'perfect', but he recurs often to the word 'fear' (i.e. fear of the Lord)[6] and the content of the Christian message is to him the 'word'.

1 Col. i, 7: ἡμῶν would appear to be the right reading. Epaphras is also a fellow-servant of Jesus Christ; δοῦλος is a title implying very close personal relationship. Like Archippus in Philem. 2, συστρατιώτης, he is a colleague of St Paul in the service of Christ.

2 I Pet. v, 1. Or is so represented, on any theory of authorship. B. H. Streeter (*The Primitive Church*) suggests that this part of the document was written by Aristion; but what authority have we for describing Aristion as an elder? He is the only name in Papias' list not so described.

3 I Pet. v, 13. Compare I Tim. i, 1, etc., γνησίῳ τέκνῳ.

4 I Pet. v, 12. Silvanus is a Latin name corresponding to Silas (cf. Saul Paulus, etc.). In Acts xv he is one of those who carried the letter containing the apostolic 'decree'; he also accompanies St Paul as far as Thessalonica and Corinth; he helps to write Thessalonians, and appears to be the carrier of, or at least the person commended in, I Peter. As the catechetical material of I Thess. iv and v has been shown to exhibit parallelisms of a remarkable order with that of I Peter i to iii, the connection with Silas may not be fortuitous.

5 See J. C. Wand on I Peter. The area is 'Pontus, Galatia, Cappadocia, Asia, and Bithynia'; there is no evidence that St Paul ever touched Pontus, Cappadocia, or Bithynia; it is unlikely that he had been in Galatia proper; he had only touched parts of Asia. It is worth remembering, too, that there are textual variations: B omits Asia. It is a kind of passage likely to receive additions. 6 Fear. See p. 68, n. 3.

9. In the case of both writers we have definite historical co-ordinates: (a) the name of a great Christian *tannā* and of subordinates in his school, (b) the name of an authoritative messenger who is presumably to carry the epistle and read it, (c) a definite group of congregations in which it is to be read, and (d) the actual contents which include catechetical material of the traditional type. The words of the epistles can only be understood in connection with this religious-social setting; by themselves they are mere libretto. They pre-suppose a school of teachers, a group of churches, a system of oral *tōrāh*, a living and complex organism of which our document is a cross-section.[1]

10. In the case of James we have no names by which to fix the tradition in time and space; but we have a strongly Jewish tradition in which the Christian teaching is described as *tōrāh* and handled by 'teachers'.

11. In the post-apostolic period the tannaite tradition appears to strengthen. It is clearly enunciated in the Pastorals[2] and I Clement.[3] St Ignatius is intensely Jewish[4] with his stress on 'discipleship' (to be made 'perfect' by martyrdom); his picture of the *ekklēsia* is based on the synagogue, the bishop taking the place of the *archisunagogos*, and presiding with the elders in the place of God (cf. Rev. iv). St Polycarp is described in the Acts of his Martyrdom as the 'teacher' of

1 This hypothesis has some kinship with the ideas underlying 'form criticism'; it regards the epistles, not as essays in literature governed by literary considerations, but as a transcript of an oral process actually going on in a particular community or series of communities. The data in the document are accepted as real data in the community. The Perdelwitz-Streeter theory is literary; it regards the document as an 'address'.

2 II Tim. ii, 1–2, etc. The Pastorals are not so much a 'church order' as a group of documents recording and defining the tannaite tradition of St Paul as it existed in a given milieu, with its true succession (γνησίῳ τέκνῳ) through Timothy and Titus. This is why the original status of the apostolic founder is established with a solemn oath, as 'herald and apostle' and '*tannā*' of the gentiles' (i, 2, 7).

3 I Clem. xlii.

4 Nothing is said by St Ignatius about submission to the ministry in the *ekklēsia* which is not said equally strongly in Jewish and Jewish-Christian documents about submission to the elders; all he does is to use the

Asia, the 'father' of the Christians.[1] Papias and Hegesippus, Basilides and Valentinus all claim to be within the didactic succession from the disciples of the Lord. In St Irenaeus the early bishops of Rome are still called 'elders'; and the Alexandrian succession of teachers goes right on (through its Caesarean offshoot) into the fourth century, culminating in St Eusebius who calls himself the 'son' of his teacher Pamphilus.

12. It must not be thought that in this chapter an attempt has been made to describe the organisation of the apostolic or sub-apostolic church, but only to draw attention to one line of thought which is likely to be sound, if, as would seem probable, Christian institutions are to be interpreted in the light of contemporary Jewish institutions, from which, in some measure, they appear to be derived.

terminology of the Christian *ekklēsia* as he knew it; and this terminology recalls the arrangement of the synagogue with the ruler in the chair of Moses and the elders round him. On the other hand the bishop has additional authority of a non-Jewish type as one 'sent', and is therefore to be regarded 'as the Lord' (Eph. vi).

1 Mart. Pol. xii, 2.

SUMMARY OF CHAPTER VIII

Colossians, addressed to the newly baptised, gives an account of St Paul's teaching function, names his subordinates, outlines the *tōrāh*, and emphasises its importance in combating heresy.

Ephesians, addressed to new gentile churches in general, gives a fuller transcript of the baptismal *tōrāh*. It insists that baptised gentiles are not to be regarded as *gērīm* (strangers) but are to be regarded 'as the homeborn' (Lev. xix, 33 ff.).

Peter does address baptised gentiles as *gērīm*. Peter A may be divided into three parts, (*a*) i, 13–ii, 10, the neo-levitical system, cf. I Thess., (*b*) ii, 11–iii, 12 ?, the social life of the community, cf. Rom. xii and xiii, (*c*) iv. 1–11, gentile behaviour (cf. Ephesians). Peter B (iv, 12 to end) is an exhortation to martyrdom; it is perhaps a separate epistle.

James is a transcript of the baptismal *tōrāh* as operated in a Jewish community. It is characterised by a highly developed pneumatic dualism.

CHAPTER VIII

THE WRITING OF THE DOCUMENTS

Colossians

1. The Colossian church must have been in an early stage of development. Epaphras, representing St Paul, seems to have founded the church; but there are other teachers, experts in the Jewish *tōrāh*, who are causing trouble by semi-gnostic teaching. He reports to St Paul, who decides to retain Epaphras at Rome and to send Tychicus in his place with a letter. It is not a free literary effort designed for publication, but an authoritative intervention in an ecclesiastical situation. It is as if he were present himself 'watching their disciplined order and firmness'.[1] The early prominence of the epistles in the canon derives from the fact that they were a powerful spiritual weapon in the hands of those who ruled and taught.

2. He points out that the surest defence against the errors of the heretics is to cling to the baptismal *tōrāh*; he goes on, if my theory is correct, to give a transcript of this *tōrāh* in a simple 'non-pauline' form, full of the atmosphere of ordinary Jewish piety, though coloured with the new spirit of the gospels.

Ephesians

3. Tychicus also took with him another document, if we accept at their face value the statements of Ephesians; but this epistle had apparently no single church in view; it was for new gentile churches, of whose foundation news had reached St Paul. The picture is that of St Paul, immobilised as a prisoner, hearing of more new churches, and still controlling them through his 'deacons' and his epistles. This general epistle, or manifesto, to the gentile church at large seems to be a new departure; but we should not think of it as a publication

---

1 Col. ii, 5: τάξιν... καὶ... στερέωμα.

in the modern sense of the word; it must have been made public by being read aloud, or used as a sourcebook of oral *tōrāh*, by authorised persons in churches which accepted St Paul as the *tannā* of the gentile world.

4. Perhaps the production of Colossians had suggested the idea of a much fuller transcript of the Pauline *tōrāh* for the benefit of gentile churches which St Paul had not seen. The message of Colossians had been the sacrificial death and high exaltation of the divine priest-king; in Ephesians this fades into the picture of his exaltation over all creation visible and invisible, and over the *ekklēsia* or church. This *ekklēsia*, though cosmic in scope, is in its earthly aspect the old Israel in its new form, a new Levitical system founded on apostles and prophets: the gentile converts are full members of the transformed Israel; nowhere else is this Pauline doctrine so fully stated.

5. Now Lev. xix, 33 f., which deals with the 'stranger that sojourneth' in the land (*gēr haggār*), extends to him the commandment of love (Lev. xix, 18) intended for the fellow-tribesman (brother): 'he shall be unto you as the home-born'.[1] But in rabbinic discussions, though the command to love the *gēr* is honourably perpetuated, he is still distinguished by the name *gēr*, which comes to mean convert. Ephesians denounces any such distinction: 'You are no longer *strangers and sojourners*, but fellow-citizens with the holy people, and *home-born*' (Eph. ii, 19). The high Pauline doctrine is thus proved from the Levitical law itself, in true Pauline style.

6. For the rest, as we have seen, it much elaborates the simple form of the baptismal pattern of Colossians, which is thereby considerably confused. The new matter is of a distinctly Pauline type, introducing the gentile taboos, the light-darkness symbolism, pneumatic dualism, and the armour of God.

---

1 The love of the fellow-tribesman is φιλαδελφία; the love of the stranger is φιλοξενία. For this pair of words, see Rom. xii, 10 and 19, Heb. xiii, 1 and 2, I Pet. iv, 8 and 9.

I Peter

7. St Peter goes contrary to Ephesians in addressing the converts as *gērīm*; but the use of the term is raised to the high religious level of strangers in the world and sojourners with God, a conception in the light of which all Israelites (Abraham himself) are *gērīm* in rabbinic tradition.

8. It is not necessary to suppose that the writer was influenced by Romans or Ephesians in order to explain any passage of Peter; but the question naturally arises whether the idea of writing the epistle, and the general form it took, may not have been suggested by the aim and scope of Ephesians, if Ephesians is prior to Peter.

9. The style of the epistle is archaic, and its author never frees himself from Jewish precedents as completely as St Paul does. The first section of material (i, 13–ii, 10) has a paschal colour,[1] but it is mainly occupied with the picture of Christianity as a new levitical system; the second section (ii, 11–iii, 12?) deals with social life, using some of the same traditional material as Rom. xii–xiii, and also encouraging unfortunate slaves with the picture of the suffering Christ, continuing that subject down to iii, 22; the third section (iv. 1–11) seems to deal with specifically gentile sins, and is vaguely reminiscent of passages in Ephesians. All three sections open with a reference to the renunciation of the *epithumia* (*yetser*) or lust.

10. The fourth section, opening iv, 12, is the one we have treated as a separate epistle (Peter B). It is, of course, doubtful whether it is so, though it certainly repeats part of the baptismal pattern; on the other hand it is not baptismal in character, but an exhortation to martyrdom (particularly addressed to the elders) which naturally follows baptismal lines, since baptism symbolises death and forecasts persecution.

1 For the paschal colour of I Peter see p. 28, n. 1.

James

11. James is addressed to the Christian (or Jewish?) world at large; the author perhaps makes no distinction. It is probably best to suppose that its intention is to give a transcript of the baptismal *tōrāh* in the school of James the brother of the Lord. It makes no mention of the problems of gentile converts or of the holiness law (though it quotes Lev. xix, 18); pure Jewish catechisms of the didactic type (like Ecclesiasticus and the *Two Ways*) seem to take this kind of *tōrāh* for granted.

12. The *Deponentes* is introduced by a biological picture of the evil inclination (*epithumia*) conceiving and bringing sin to birth, and sin coming to maturity and producing death; this is balanced by a picture of the 'word' (*logos*) by which the Father of lights causes us to be born as a 'firstfruits' of his creations. The hearer is then urged to receive the word with meekness and silence, and to be a doer of the work.[1] This contrast of word and work introduces the exposition of the *tōrāh* of love and the extended discourse on faith and works.

13. Passing over the command 'not to be many teachers' and its pendant discourse on the tongue, we return to the pattern.

The wise man will show his wisdom by his good 'walking', a phrase which introduces the contrast of the two wisdoms, the one a heavenly *pneuma*, the other 'earthy, psychic, daemonic'. This is followed by a section on the *hēdonai* (delights) which carry on war in our members, causing fighting, robbery, etc.; they are ultimately summed up in the 'spirit which God caused to dwell in us, which lusteth unto envy'. (The rabbi does not hesitate to say that the evil disposition, *yetser*, was created by God.) The *Subiecti*, etc. now follow.

14. Our analysis only covers Jas. i, 1–iv, 12; the rest is material foreign to our pattern.

1 The λόγος-ἔργον antithesis is common; ἀκροατής, 'hearer' (Jas. i, 23, Rom. ii, 13), is perhaps a technical term for a catechumen. The emphasis on hearing and doing marks the close of Lev. xix and also of the Sermon on the Mount. Compare Jas. i, 22 with John xiii, 17. All these passages seem to echo one sentiment.

CHAPTER IX

THE RECEPTION OF THE WORD

SUMMARY OF CHAPTER IX

All *tōrāh* opens with an ethical dualism of which the most primitive form is to turn from idols to serve a living and true God.

Pneumatic dualism distinguishes either (*a*) the man's own *nephesh* from his (evil) inclination (*yetser*, *epithumia*), or (*b*) the Holy Spirit from the devil; confused forms are common. Various forms of Renunciation in the catholic baptismal rites.

The same type of thought regards such concepts as word, wisdom, truth, as *pneumata* or *dunameis*, vitalising actualities of divine origin or nature.

The Word in New Testament *tōrāh*. Its reception (baptism) as re-enactment of creation, new birth, or the sowing of a seed.

Deponentes suggests that the unclothing (and clothing) at baptism has acquired a symbolic meaning. (The cup of milk; unction.)

The act of worship: Abba father: tongues.

Subiecti suggests a bow or prostration. The divine presence in the *ekklēsia*, especially in the elders.

Vigilate seems to renew the caution as to temptation.

State suggests a command to stand either (*a*) in prayer, or (*b*), more probably, upright and perfect, a possible rabbinic climax.

Resistite, with its apocalyptic colour, is more characteristically Christian, and carries on the thought of the onset of temptation or persecution.

In Ephesians the devil is to be actively fought with the Word.

THE RECEPTION OF THE WORD

1. In this chapter we assume the existence of the common pattern and attempt an interpretation along baptismal lines.

2. All forms of the *tōrāh* begin from some kind of dualism, to judge between clean and unclean,[1] to eschew evil and do good,[2] to put off falsehood and speak truth,[3] and so on. The earliest form of this dualism is to turn from idols to serve a living and true God,[4] and to abandon the unholy in order to associate with the holy. The convert, in Paul, comes out of darkness (an unclean world in which he had served vanities) to enter the *ekklēsia*, or circle of light, which the Holy Spirit indwells. Even the ethical catechisms like Ecclesiasticus and James have their existence within a consecrated community of the levitical type, just as in the English catechism the 'duties' appear in the heart of a sacramental order.

3. Long before Christianity, the holy-unholy category had been applied to the inward life. There is light and darkness in the soul[5] (spirit and flesh as St Paul rashly called them in

1 This is the function of the elders according to *Mekilta* to Exod. xviii; the possession of discrimination ('understanding') is necessary before a person *can* depart from evil, which is the first step in the fear of the Lord.

2 Ps. xxxiv, 14.

3 Eph. iv, 25.

4 I Thess. i, 9, Acts xiii, 14: the basic idea of all Jewish *tōrāh* both in theory and in historic origin. The original antithesis to the fear of the Lord is given in the second commandment; it is the *Abodah Zarah*, the foreign worship. All evil, therefore, is a kind of idolatry.

5 The symbolism of light and darkness in Paul and John is probably a development of the ideas of holy and unholy. The section of the Mishnah which deals with pure and impure is called *Tohāroth*, which means etymologically 'illuminations'. The use of the word illumination for baptism may, therefore, have a Jewish ancestry. A levitical form of the light-darkness *tōrāh* is found in II Cor. vi, 14–18, which closely resembles Test. Levi, xix, 1. The only light-darkness verse in I Peter is part of the levitical sanctuary section (ii, 9).

Galatians) and these are contrary the one to the other;[1] but earlier still was the thought of the pure and holy spirit which God breathed into man,[2] and the evil inclination, with which it had to contend. The conception is sometimes little more than a mere dualistic psychology, but in its most dramatic form it becomes a contention within the soul between the Holy Spirit of God and the dark spirit of evil which is dramatised as the devil or Satan, a contention which is itself only a focal point in the cosmic battle between God's forces of light and those evil forces which possess the world. All these conceptions find their place in the various forms of the baptismal pattern, and are eventually crystallised into the Renunciation which precedes the catholic baptismal rite.[3]

4. Pneumatic dualism arises in a thought world in which a quasi-sensual reality is attributed to what we tend to regard as abstractions. The soul (*nephesh*) or spirit (*rūah*) is such a reality; so is the evil inclination (*yetser*); in *Testaments* what appear to be abstract vices and virtues are also called spirits (*pneumata*). The same realistic interpretation holds good of words like wisdom, word, knowledge, *tōrāh*, and even fear of the Lord. To put it shortly, they imply a real presence of God. They may be thought of as God acting in the holy community, or as powers proceeding from God. The learner is actually approaching the divine presence;[4] where the *tōrāh* is spoken of, there is the *Shekīnāh* itself.[5]

5. The best-known example of a *dunamis* of this kind in the didactic tradition is that of *hokmāh* (wisdom); in the New Testament the term 'Word' (Aramaic, *memrā*) practically takes

---

1 Matt. vi, 22–23 is a striking example.

2 See p. 27, n. 1.

3 The catholic 'Renunciation' usually specifies the devil, the world, and the flesh, and often includes the word vanity, which we have connected with idolatry. In its earliest forms it obviously carries with it renunciation of pagan cults, the gods being regarded as devils. By the flesh is meant, of course, the 'inclination'. The world is more suggestive of the Johannine books; but see Jas. iv, 4.

4 E.g. Ecclus. i and ii.

5 E.g. *Pirke Aboth* iv, 12. See p. 9 and notes.

its place; and in his baptismal prologue to the gospel, St John in every respect assimilates the concept to that of wisdom.[1] The Word is a creative *dunamis* proceeding from God, producing light, life, and the whole cosmos; it is present and active in the proclamation of the Christian message, and, as in the creation story, it is accompanied by the Spirit. In receiving the Word, the believer is taking into his inward being light and fertility (seed) as well as truth; a process of generation or creation is begun which has the power to 'save his soul', that is to preserve in purity the *nephesh* he received at his natural birth.

6. It is very natural, then, that there should cluster round the *Deponentes* a series of formulae based on the following ideas: (*a*) a re-enactment of the creation myth,[2] (*b*) a new-birth, and the thought of the converts as children, and (*c*) the sowing of a seed.[3] In the Jewish rite there was a reference to creation by a word at this point, and the baptised were said to be as little children.[4]

7. The *Deponentes* itself appears to be based on the stripping

---

1 It is possible to go too far in crediting the author of the fourth gospel with a special *logos*-philosophy of his own; the prologue follows step by step the same lines as the Wisdom-prologue of Ecclesiasticus, until it reaches its characteristic statement of the incarnation of the *logos*. i, 12–13 is another form of the formula preceding the *Deponentes* in James and I Peter. See also Wisdom vii, 22, xviii, 14, etc.

2 The explicit connection of word-light in the creation myth of Gen. i with word-light received in baptism through evangelisation is made not only in John, but in Paul. In II Cor. iv, 6, after referring to his handling of the ministry of the 'word of God', and describing it as the 'illumination of the glory of the Christ who is the image of God', he goes on to say, 'It is the God who said, Out of darkness light shall shine (Gen. i, 2), who has shone in our hearts unto the illumination of the knowledge of the glory of God in the face (presence?) of Christ.'

3 It has not been found possible within the limits of this book to develop the second baptismal motif of assimilation to the divine priest-king (Christ) risen from the dead, which obviously exists in such phrases as 'clothe yourselves with Christ'. The idea is especially characteristic of Paul.

4 But there does not appear to be any evidence that, in the Jewish rite, the *gēr* was new-created or reborn. See, however, Gen. R. xxxix, 4, 'whoever brings a heathen near to God and converts him is as though he had created him'.

off of garments which preceded immersion.[1] In Paul we find formulae based on the reclothing,[2] and the terminology suggests that the assumption of a new (white?) robe may already have acquired some ceremonial significance; the references to the washing of clothes and the new robe in Revelation suggest a similar cycle of ideas, and may be based on the ceremonies for the consecration and purification of priests.

8. Similarly the references to milk are to be connected with the cup of milk (and honey) given in the later rituals. The addition of honey is found as early as Barnabas (vi, 17). It would be natural to clothe the candidate and give him a drink immediately after immersion. A third natural accompaniment, anointing, leaves no mark in New Testament thought except perhaps in I John (ii, 27); as a religious rite it was strange to the Greek mind, and took some time to establish itself.

9. All our documents now refer to an act of worship which may be expressed in terms of a transformation of the levitical system of sacrifice. The new member of the brotherhood 'calls on God as Father'.[3] A well-known baptismal formula in Galatians and Romans[4] gives the first utterance after the reception of the Spirit as '*Abba*' (father). The use of this Aramaic word may be connected with the gift of tongues which succeeds baptism in Acts, and was addressed to God; or with the 'Our Father', the recital of which became a feature of the later baptismal rite.[5] In some way, at any rate, the convert

---

1 While no New Testament text is sufficient to prove that the method of baptism was by total immersion, the precedent of Jewish practice renders it likely that such immersion was the general rule.

2 These formulae may tentatively be connected with the king ritual, as may the 'armour' passages, of which there is one faint trace in I Peter (iv, 1). See p. 86, n. 1.

3 I Pet. i, 17. We may, perhaps, connect this with the invocation of the name in Jas. ii, 7; but the verb here is in the passive voice and suggests that a name was invoked over the neophyte by the minister of baptism.

4 Gal. iv, 6, Rom. viii, 15.

5 When did the 'laying on of hands' come? There is an interval in Acts viii, 17; but was this normal? In xix, 6 it would appear to be part of the baptismal rite, the part, namely, when the Spirit was received, and

enters into the high eucharistic worship addressed by the church to God.

10. The *Subiecti* demands subordination (we may, perhaps, conjecture a bow or prostration) not only to God, but to the elders or fathers who rule the holy community with divine authority. The sons of God must learn the rule of humility and mutual subordination which animates the brotherhood in which the presence dwells.

11. The *Vigilate* is in the nature of a caution and may be taken in close connection with the next phrase, *State* (stand); compare I Cor. xvi, 13 'Watch ye, stand firm', or x, 12 'let him that thinketh he standeth take heed lest he fall'. The word *grēgorein* (watch) in the Gethsemane story is connected with temptation, while in Q and Mark xiii it has to do with the afflictions which precede the coming of the Kingdom. It would appear, then, that the newly baptised brother is again warned of temptations and afflictions to come. The pattern story of the baptism of our Lord is also followed by a temptation by Satan.

12. The *State* is a command to stand, possibly to stand up after a prostration. It is the posture of prayer (which links this section with the preceding); but it may also imply standing upright and firm in the word which has been received; it is the posture of the righteous man. It should be remembered that in the ancient world entrance into a sanctuary or into the presence of a divine being was marked by ablution, putting on special clothes, prostration, and then standing up to pray. The new Christian may thus have made his entry into the *ekklēsia* or sanctuary of the Holy Spirit.

13. Our three major authorities, Ephesians, Peter, and James, exhibit a stronger form of the *State* in the *Resistite*, or command to withstand the devil, which assumes in Ephesians a lyrical and dramatic form, based on a light-darkness

inspired utterance expected. Laying on of hands is closely linked with 'baptisms' (τε) in Heb. vi, 2. It would harmonise well with counsels to humble oneself and be subordinate.

cosmology, which is anticipated in certain sections of that epistle, which are not found in Colossians, though they have clear parallels in I Thessalonians and Romans. These non-Colossian passages in Ephesians belong to a type of *tōrāh* represented in *Testaments* and Hermas; in fact the correlatives 'neither give place to the devil' and 'grieve not the Holy Spirit' can hardly be explained without using Hermas; the last of the *Mandata* makes use of the whole vocabulary, light and darkness, good or evil *epithumia*, devil and Holy Spirit, and clothing oneself with armour.[1] But this elaborate development of Hebrew dualistic thought does not seem to be characteristic of the common pattern.

14. James presents a psychological pneumatic dualism, of a type which Paul also makes use of in Galatians and I Corinthians, though this would not, in so elaborate a form, appear to be characteristic of the common pattern.

15. If we rely on what is common to all our documents, we are left with something closer to the old piety of Ecclesiasticus and to the terminology of the synoptic gospels—humble yourselves, watch, pray, stand firm. In *Testaments*, the synoptics, and rabbinic theology generally, the devil (Beliar, Satan) is the enemy within the soul; in fact there is a rabbinic saying to the effect that Satan, the *yetser*, and the angel of death are all names for the same thing. If this is the last word, the pattern ends, like the Lord's Prayer, with the evil one.

1 Lack of space prevents adequate treatment of these passages, which I believe are to be connected with the king ritual and with a light-darkness cosmology of the Iranian type. (*a*) The 'panoply' is the regalia of Jehovah himself, Isa. lix, 17, Wisdom v, 16, etc.; (*b*) the place of the king in the Hebrew state was taken by the high-priest who was the anointed of Jehovah and his representative: the annual renewal ritual of the sacred priest-king being found in the so-called Day of Atonement ritual which 'Aaron' has to undergo 'lest he die'; (*c*) in the making or renewal of a high priest, the important point, after immersion, sacrifice, and the anointing either with blood or oil, is clothing in the regalia: this clothing and crowning being given a spiritual meaning in Test. Levi viii, which closely approximates to the panoply passage in Ephesians; (*d*) Christ, the 'anointed', or divine priest-king, is pictured as so crowned and clothed, though with sword and crown (and armour) after the fashion of David (Ps. xlv) (or Melchizedek?): Heb. ii, 4, Rev. i, 9 ff., etc.

16. But Ephesians itself comes back to a word which we have seen to be highly characteristic of the pattern. After describing the defensive armour which it calls the *panoplia* of God, it refers to one offensive weapon only, the sword of the Spirit, which is the Word of God.[1] It might be that in the pattern the Word which had been received by the believer was the true antithesis of the enemy power in the soul. As the *epithumia* made war against the soul, so the Word of truth had power to save it. 'I write unto you, young men,' says St John, 'because ye are strong, and the Word of God abides in you, and ye have conquered the evil one.'

The Word of God is what is received in baptism; it comes with creative power; it regenerates. In vigil and prayer it is referred to continually, and it is the sword by which the believer overcomes the evil.

In the pattern story with which the gospel opens, the Lord receives a word from heaven at his baptism, and then overcomes the evil one with the Word in his forty days of temptation.[2]

[1] The 'word' as a sword seems to be a common piece of symbolism; cf. Wisdom xviii, 16, Heb. iv, 12, Rev. i, 16, xix, 15.
[2] In connection with this exposition of the *logos* philosophy, see Rendel Harris, *The Origin of the Prologue to St John's Gospel*.

CONCLUSION

1. It has been shown that a series of formulae appears in each of the documents examined, usually in the same order.

2. An attempt has been made to show that this series of formulae can be treated as if it belonged to a pattern which had an independent existence apart from the documents which embody it.

3. On this assumption an examination was made of the terminology attributed to the pattern; and this examination made it likely that it was connected with baptismal and catechetical procedure.

4. The characteristic divergences of thought and style in the different documents are explained by the hypothesis that this procedure was oral.

5. To illustrate this hypothesis, reference has been made to documentary evidence bearing on oral instruction in the religious-social community, both in Judaism and Christianity.

We are a long way, however (granted the truth of the whole theory), from any reconstruction or complete survey of a pre-literary Christian catechism.

1. The examination has been limited to those parts of four documents which exhibit similarity of content and order.

2. The points to which attention has been specifically directed are usually those which all four exhibit in a striking degree. All that could be done was to gain some idea of the original pattern in so far as this method brings it into view; but the points which all four documents agree in retaining may only provide a dim vision of part of it. Subject to these limitations, I think that four opinions may be offered which bear on its origin.

1. As no specific instruction for gentiles can safely be attributed to it, it may have originated in a Jewish community.

CONCLUSION

2. As the order of formulae recovered cannot be found in pure Jewish documents, or even in the *Two Ways* or Hermas, it may have assumed its present form in the Christian church.

3. The indications in Thessalonians, Corinthians, and Romans suggest that it may even then have been used in the Pauline school in a form which had been adapted for use in the gentile mission, so that its formation may perhaps be traced to a Jewish Christian church previous to A.D. 50. St Paul makes it quite clear that whatever traditions he had were not his own, but received by him.

4. On the whole it suggests the atmosphere of the old Jewish piety in which the first Christianity arose.

As to its purpose, the connection with baptism seems clear; but whether it is a didactic catechism to be learned before or after baptism, or whether it is in the nature of a baptism ritual (as suggested in Chapter IX), or whether it partakes of both natures, and provides a pattern of sound words for either,[1] will not be established without further study not only of the New Testament, but also of rabbinic and subapostolic authorities.

---

1 That this is possible is shown by the fact that in Jewish proselyte baptism various 'commandments' were recited during the ceremony. Such a practice may be alluded to by St Ignatius (Rom. iii, 1), 'the things you command when you make disciples'. I John, as we have seen, seems to connect the reception of the commandments with baptism; and so perhaps does Matt. xxviii, 19. To 'make disciples' appears to mean to baptise; if this usage of words is taken over from rabbinic practice, it may be that reception into the rabbinic school was accompanied by *tebīlāh*.

TABLE VII. Outline of the pattern.

1. *Introductory.*
   (*a*) *Neo-levitical.* (For gentiles, cf. Lev. xvii–xix.)
       No longer to walk as the gentiles in vanity (i.e. idolatry, etc.).
       To avoid the (three) great sins against holy living.
       Consecration: brotherly love.
   (*b*) *Rabbinic* (cf. Ecclus. ii, etc.).
       Faith, hope, endurance (and love).
       To endure afflictions and temptations (with joy).
       To resist the evil inclination (lust) which makes war against the soul.

2. *The Word.*
   (Compare Wisdom in the Wisdom literature.)
   The word of truth is able to save your souls.
   New birth by the word of truth (of life, etc.). In Paul the new creation.
   The word as seed.
   Converts regarded as infants who must grow in wisdom till they reach
       perfection (maturity).

3. *The Baptismal Paraenesis.*
   Wherefore, putting off all evil and falsehood (Ps. xxxiv, 13): receive the
       word (milk): as children of God:
   exhibit the virtues of a learner (meekness, truth, etc.):
   offer pure (spiritual) worship to the Father (Mal. i, 11?).
   Submit yourselves to God, to the elders, to one another:
   humble yourselves:
   watch and pray (for the word):
   stand firm:
   resist the devil.

Note. It must not be assumed that any original document existed of
which this is an outline, though it is not impossible that this is the case.
It may more probably represent (in a mutilated form) a series of formulae
which tended to be employed in dealing with candidates for baptism in the
various apostolic traditions, and derived from an original mode of procedure
which spread widely through the New Testament church and developed
along divergent lines.

APPENDIX I

PLINY'S LETTER

If the theory advanced in this book has any validity, some trace of the actual procedure might have been expected to survive. It is possible that this is to be found in the information given to Pliny as to Christian procedure early in the first century; this information does not refer to the eucharist which he says took place later. The text reads:

Stato die	τακτῇ ἡμέρᾳ
ante lucem convenire,	πρωὶ συνελθεῖν,
carmenque Christo	ψαλμὸν δὲ τῷ Χριστῷ
quasi deo	ὡς θεῷ
dicere secum invicem,	λέγειν ἐν ἑαυτοῖς ἀντίφωνον,
seque sacramento	ἑαυτοὺς δὲ ὅρκῳ
non in scelus aliquod obstringere,	οὐκ εἰς ἀδικίαν τινὰ ἀναθεματίζειν,
sed ne furta,	ἀλλὰ μὴ κλέμματα,
ne latrocinia,	μὴ ἅρπαγας,
ne adulteria committerent,	μὴ πορνείας ποιεῖν,
ne fidem fallerent,	μηδὲ τὴν πίστιν ψεύδεσθαι,
ne depositum appellati	μηδὲ τὴν παραθήκην ἐγκλη-
abnegarent.	θέντες ἀπαρνήσασθαι.

C. Plini et Traiani *Ep.* 96, 97.

I have ventured to suggest in a second column the possible Greek equivalent of the Latin text, which reads exactly like the catechetical material in the Jewish and Judaeo-Christian literature. It is possible that the 'depositum' may represent the 'deposit' of faith, and that the words may be a fragment of a catechetical or baptismal ritual. What took place was first the antiphonal recitation of a 'carmen' to Christ as God, that is, something in the way of a declaration of faith; and secondly, the taking of an oath to abstain from certain sins, and to be true to the faith.

What should this be but baptism? or something connected with baptism?

In Aristides, we find first a credal statement with regard to faith in Christ, and then an outline of the moral life such as we have here, or find in the *Two Ways*. It contains the clause 'they do not deny a deposit'; but this is only found in the Syriac version; it must certainly be taken literally here.

⟨ 91 ⟩

THE COLOSSIAN CATECHISM

No attempt has been made to 'reconstruct' the text of a primitive apostolic catechism (or baptismal ritual); the most that can be found is a common plan or pattern with a common thought sequence and certain common phrases. On the other hand, it has been noted that the Colossian catechism does not exhibit certain characteristic 'Pauline' notes which are found in Ephesians, Romans, and Thessalonians, and even in I Peter; without denying that some of these may belong to the Christian mission preaching as a whole, it may well be that Colossians provides a primitive version of the teaching. A still purer text may be made by omitting from Colossians certain formulae which we have every reason to suppose are characteristic of Paul, being found in Paul only, and occurring either at a different point in the corresponding passage in Ephesians, or even in another epistle.

In order to reconstruct a basic Colossian catechism, I have cut out these passages; the following is what remains:

Levitical Prologue...fornication, uncleanness, passion, evil inclination, and covetousness, which is idolatry; through which comes the anger of God; in which you also walked once, when you lived in these.   iii, 5–7.

Deponentes.

And now put off also all anger, wrath, evil, slander, shameful speaking, out of your mouth:

Lie not to one another...   iii, 8.

Put on, as the chosen of God, holy and beloved, bowels of mercy, kindness, lowliness, meekness, longsuffering;

Forbearing one another and forgiving one another;

As the Lord forgave you, so also do you yourselves;

In addition to all these, the love which is the bond of perfection;

And let the peace of Christ reign in your hearts, into which you have been called, in one body;

And be thankful... (The word of Christ dwell in you richly in all knowledge)...teaching and admonishing one another in psalms and hymns and spiritual songs, singing with grace in your hearts to God;

And whatever you do, whether in word or deed, all in the Name of the Lord Jesus;

Giving thanks to God the Father through him.   iii, 12–17.

APPENDIX II

Subiecti.

Women, be subject to your husbands as is fitting in the Lord;

Men, love your wives, and do not be bitter against them;

Children, obey your parents in all things, for this is pleasing in the Lord;

Fathers, provoke not your children, lest they be discouraged;

Slaves, obey in all things your masters according to the flesh, not with eye-service as men-pleasers, but in singleness of heart, fearing the Lord; whatever you do, work heartily, as for the Lord and not for men, knowing that from the Lord you will receive the reward of inheritance; be slaves of the Lord Christ; for he who does wrong will be repaid for his wrongdoing; and there is no respect of persons.

Masters, afford your slaves what is right and fair, knowing that you also have a master.   iii, 18–iv, 1.

Vigilate.

In prayer persevere, watching thereto with thanksgiving;

Praying also at the same time for us, that God may open to us the door of the word.   iv, 2–3.

Walk in wisdom with regard to those outside, redeeming the time;

Your word always in grace, seasoned with salt: to know how you ought to make answer to everyone.   iv, 5.

State.

Epaphras salutes you, one of yourselves, a servant of Christ Jesus;

Ever in strife on your behalf in his prayers, that you may stand perfect and fulfilled in all the will of God.   iv, 13.

APPENDIX III

THE MATTHAEAN SERMON ON THE MOUNT

A few notes only can be given to justify the statement that the
Matthaean Sermon on the Mount is in essence a handling of Jewish
tōrāh which has an ultimate levitical or rabbinic base. The present
treatment omits from consideration Chapter vi and a few other
passages which, on critical grounds, cannot be regarded as parts of
the original document; even so it can only touch on a few obvious
points.

Introductory (v, 1–16). The Beatitudes (especially those peculiar to Matthew) emphasise some of the virtues which are usually
impressed on learners at the opening of any Jewish catechism; the
poor, the meek, the peaceful. There is, of course, vastly more than
appears in any Jewish catechism.

The usual counsel as to 'temptation' is transformed into the
command to rejoice under persecution, and this note, as we have
seen, is echoed in Paul, Peter, and James. The opening of Peter B
(iv, 12 ff.) must actually be based on this passage; and Peter A in
ii, 12 is clearly based on v, 16.

The Jewish Law (17–20). This section expresses the highest
possible opinion of the sacredness of the old *tōrāh*, and states that, so
far from destroying it, the new *tōrāh* of the gospel is actually ful-
filling it, that is, bringing it to its mature and perfect state.

The Five Commandments (21–48). This section is based on a
consideration of five commandments, each of which is prefaced by
an appeal to the common oral teaching: 'Ye have heard that it was
said.' In two cases it reads, 'Ye have heard that it was said unto the
ancients' (i.e. men of old time, or possibly the elders).

To what is reference being made?

The first two commandments dealt with are from the decalogue,
being the first two of the second table. The third may be from
Num. xxx, 2, Deut. xxiii, 21, or Lev. xix, 12; of these Lev. xix is far
the more likely source for popular oral teaching. The fourth is from
Exod. xxi, 24 or Lev. xxiv, 20. The fifth is from Lev. xix, 18. It
seems, therefore, that two of the commandments dealt with are
taken from the decalogue, and the remainder from the Holiness
Code. This is fully in accordance with rabbinic custom; in *Mekilta*
to Exod. xiii, 8, for instance, which deals with Joseph as a pattern
of the ten commandments, it adds three more to the ten, all taken
from the Law of Holiness: Lev. xix, 17, 'Thou shalt not hate';
Lev. xix, 18, 'Thou shalt not revenge thyself'; Lev. xxv, 36, 'and
thy brother shall live by thee'. It is precisely such additional
commandments which form the basis of the Sermon on the Mount.

In working from an eclectic group of commandments drawn from
the decalogue and the Law of Holiness, therefore, our Lord is only

doing what other Jewish teachers did; and as he actually appeals to some form of oral instruction known to his hearers, it is to be presumed that he did not himself compose this eclectic group.

The fifth of the commandments is quoted in a non-biblical form, 'Thou shalt love thy neighbour, and hate thine enemy.' Travers Herford (*Talmud and Apocrypha*) makes the point that any bystander could have corrected our Lord, as the Law of Moses nowhere says this. The Lord does not quote this saying as from the Law of Moses, but only as from the system of oral instruction familiar to his hearers: 'Ye have heard that it was said.' We must presume, I think, that the commandment, as quoted, did exist in some well-known oral system, familiar to him and to his hearers; and, if this is the case, it is fair to presume that it is from this oral system that the whole set of commandments is taken.

Now in one version of the *Two Ways* (or *Way of Life*), which is an actual Jewish catechism of the period, we find the command: 'Unto the end thou shalt hate him who is evil' (Barn. xix, 11), though this is omitted, or even corrected, in the other version, which says, 'Thou shalt not hate any man' (Did. ii, 7).

But the *Way of Life* provides a catechism exactly of the kind we want; for it opens, like the Sermon on the Mount, not only with an emphasis on the catechumen virtues of meekness and quietness, but also with a series of prohibitions of an eclectic type, many of them taken from the Law of Holiness. The conviction grows, therefore, that the Lord was working from such a catechism, and that it may well have contained the command to hate one's enemy.

How, then, does he handle this catechism? The answer is in the first instance by further appeal to the Law of Moses.

In the case of murder he brings in from the Law of Holiness the prohibition of hatred (Lev. xix, 17), which he regards as an equally grave sin. In the case of the seventh commandment (adultery), he brings in the ninth (the lawless desire). In a subsection of this passage he deals with the provision for divorce (Deut. xxiv, 1); but his complete prohibition of divorce had apparently been anticipated in Samaritan *tōrāh*, and in the *tōrāh* of the *Zadokite Fragment*, and had always been binding on the priesthood. In the same way, the *Zadokite Fragment* appears to prohibit oaths.

The transformation of the law of retaliation into a retaliation of good for evil reaches a height of sublimity untouched before; but the counsel to turn the cheek to the smiter is anticipated in Isa. l, 6. The levitical command to love your neighbour as yourself is extended to cover one's enemy in a full and explicit manner which is quite new; but the idea is to be found in the Old Testament, for instance, in the stories of Joseph and David. In these cases we do not do justice to Judaism unless we realise that our Lord meant what he said in the statement that his teaching was merely bringing to fullness and maturity what was in the law already.

This passage reaches its climax in the aphorism 'Be ye therefore perfect as your Father in heaven is perfect', or in Luke, 'Be ye therefore merciful, etc.' These aphorisms, according to Hertz (*Pentateuch and Haftorahs*) were in vogue among the Rabbis as paraphrases of the central saying of the Holiness Code, 'Ye shall be holy; for I the Lord your God am holy' (xix, 2).

The command not to judge (vii, 1) is probably part of the Sermon; it is to be noted that it is cast in the same mock-retaliatory style as v, 43-48, which perhaps it should immediately follow. Lev. xix, 15 commands righteous judgment, a command which may have formed the basis for this saying.

I am inclined to think that the next verse, which really belongs to the Matthaean Sermon on the Mount, is vii, 12, the enunciation of the Golden Rule, which sums up all the teaching we have just been considering. The Golden Rule in its negative form was already familiar to the Jews, being found in Tobit (iv, 15) and taught by Hillel. The positive form involves, however, radically new consequences. Both repose on Lev. xxiv, 19; see p. 17, n. 1.

This, he says, is the law and the prophets, and so concludes his exposition of the law.

Conclusion. The imagery of the *Two Ways* (vii, 13-14) is, of course, a commonplace of nearly all Jewish catechisms (cf. Prov. iv, 18, 19).

The warning against false prophets (vii, 13 ff.) represents perhaps a natural caution against wrong teaching such as might be found at the end of any outline of instruction, and is found at the end of the *Way of Life* (Did. vi and xi).

This section passes into a caution on doing, as well as saying (vii, 21) or merely hearing (vii, 24); such an emphasis may perhaps be found in the last verse of Lev. xix, and is certainly echoed in Jas. i, 22, Rom. ii, 13, John xiii, 17, etc. See p. 78, n. 1.

Most Hebrew codes end with an epilogue of a prophetic nature saying what will happen to those who obey and those who do not obey the law. In this case it takes the form of the parable of the two builders; there are three points which serve to illustrate how completely this document remains within the intellectual limits of the old *tōrāh*: (1) the contrast is the old one of the 'wise' and the 'fool'; (2) the wise man is he who 'hears and does the words'; (3) there is no suggestion of rewards and punishments in a future life.

The Sermon on the Mount is the perfection of the old *tōrāh*. We may even see in our Lord the champion of the old Jewish piety against the new piety of the Pharisees which was destined to colour the religion of Israel.

Printed in the United States
By Bookmasters